Pamela Reif

YOU DESERVE THIS

PAMELA REIF

YOU DESERVE THIS

Simple & Natural Recipes for a Healthy Lifestyle

Bowl Cookbook

Community EDITIONS

PROLOGUE

'Listen to your body, it knows what it needs.'
... but are we really listening or are we just hearing what we want to hear?

My name is Pamela, I was born in July 9, 1996 and I grew up in Germany. People would have described me as a responsible, well-balanced and overall super-happy child. I still consider this to be true and accurate today. Especially these days when everything is so fast paced, with countless (potential) stress factors (often unnecessary, by the way). I am very glad that I have kept those character traits.

My job is sharing my life, my interests and thoughts with people from all around the world and, by doing that, motivating them to pursue a healthier lifestyle. At the age of 16 I began sharing pictures of myself on social media. Today my community on Instagram and YouTube has grown to 5 million people. How many people is that? I can't imagine. I simply consider myself extremely lucky that somewhere on this beautiful planet people are doing my fitness exercises, enjoying my recipes and feeling motivated to achieve a healthier physical feeling.

SO WHY A COOKBOOK?

Aren't there enough cookbooks already? Well, yeah, maybe. I would never claim that my book is soooooo much better than all the other ones on the market. I'm glad if every passionate person becomes successful in life. But in this book I'd like to address everyone who wants to treat his or her body well. Everyone who wants to give it what it needs and deserves. All the recipes were put together by me. I've cooked, served and taken the pictures myself – and I ate and finished every single dish. Where professional food photographers add, for example, hairspray or glue to add some shine or glossiness, I have only used natural products like olive oil. The pictures of me were taken by my photographer and friend Anna. So I decided to take three dedicated weeks off from 'normal' life to produce all the content for this book. And then ... three weeks turned into one year. A long-term project I had totally underestimated. But at the same time a project dear to my heart that grew more important to me than any of my other projects. I wrote the texts for the recipes on flights to the United States, was in dialogue with my publisher somewhere on the road in Germany and edited the pictures on lonely nights at my desk. It was important to me to create this cookbook myself.

The English translation was written by my brother Dennis and afterwards checked by me. Again, I thought it's nicer if we do it ourselves. If you spot a mistake or if something sounds 'weird' to you – I'll take the blame. I was also unfamiliar with two or three British phrases, so I just went for the American version. And to make this book even more 'international' I decided to keep some wonderful German words like 'Kaiserschmarrn' (it's shredded pancakes) on purpose. Hope you don't mind!

To cut a long story short: by me, for you. For a balanced, healthy life full of energy and happiness. Because you deserve this!

CONTENT

ABBREVIATIONS

mg	milligram
g	gram
kg	kilogram
kcal	kilocalories: the energy required to raise the temperature of 1 litre of water by 1°C. Generally used to give us an idea of how much 'energy' a food provides us. Each person needs an individual amount of energy each day; for women it's usually between 1600–2500 kcal.
µg	microgram
ml	millilitre
l	litre
pH	The pH is a scale used to specify how acidic or alkaline a water-based solution is. Acidic solutions have a lower pH, while alkaline solutions have a higher pH.
tsp	teaspoon (the small ones)
tbsp	tablespoon (the regular ones)
ORAC scale	The ORAC scale (Oxygen Radical Absorbance Capacity) is used to measure the antioxidant capacity of foods.

Important information about this book

As a rule, the *ingredient amounts* per recipe make enough for one bowl. If not, I will make sure to tell you. The diameter of my bowls is generally 17–20cm, and for the sweet bowls 12–15cm. I recommend using *accurate kitchen scales*, as for a lot of recipes using the precise amounts can make a big difference to the result.

Unless otherwise stated, the *nutritional values* refers to one serving, and therefore one bowl. I have included the toppings in the calculation. Optional ingredients are not counted.

There's a *preparation time* for each individual dish, which makes it easier for you to estimate how long you will need to make the recipe. This includes the preparation, resting, baking and cooking time.

Whenever *baking in the oven* I always use the convection or fan mode.

I often use a *food processor*, this refers to a kitchen appliance that can shred, purée and grate ingredients. It's not a blender.

Some might define bowl recipes solely as so-called one-pot dishes that can be prepared in the bowl itself, without the use of any *kitchen aids like pans or the oven*. However, I love the flavours and various possibilities offered by roasting and baking though, and that's why I defined the term 'bowl recipe' a little broader in my book.

All product recommendations in this book are based on my personal opinion and have not been sponsored.

Vegetarian: All recipes that don't include fish or meat carry this icon. Honey can easily be swapped with vegan alternatives like agave syrup or date syrup.

Vegan: If you say no to all animal products like fish, meat, dairy or eggs, you can find a lot of suitable dishes with this icon.

Dairy-free: Vegans, some vegetarians and lactose-intolerant people take a pass on cow's milk and its products. Since I barely use dairy products, you can find a big variety of dairy-free dishes in this book.

Gluten-free: If you're suffering from coeliac disease, or are gluten-sensitive, you should look out for this icon. You can easily substitute grains containing gluten with pseudo-cereals like quinoa or buckwheat. Most of my recipes are gluten-free though.

HOLD YOUR BOWL – APPRECIATE IT WITH ALL SENSES
APPETIZING PRESENTATION
DISHES ARE OFTEN FLEXIBLE AND INGREDIENTS CAN BE SUBSTITUTED
BOWLS
ARE AVAILABLE IN BEAUTIFUL COLOURS AND PATTERNS
AN EASY CONCEPT – BASE + TOPPINGS
CONSCIOUS CONSUMPTION
IDEAL SERVING SIZE FOR 1 PERSON
SIMPLE RECIPES AND SHORT COOKING TIME
INSPIRED BY BUDDHISM
TEXTURES AND FLAVOURS BLEND TOGETHER

INTRODUCTION

'You Deserve This' ... but what do I actually deserve?

Do you know what's a huge waste? Not enjoying your precious life in the very best ways possible. By that, I am not referring to the short minutes of enjoying a pizza or a bar of chocolate. Is someone raising an eyebrow? I'd understand that. We are always looking for instant satisfaction. Something that provides us with a quick high but – if we're being honest – drags us down a little lower physically and mentally right afterwards. Not everyone feels guilty after having a burger – you shouldn't anyway. But when 'occasionally' turns into 'daily', the brief moment of joy quickly vanishes ... we get used to it too quickly. We also suffer from constant fatigue, lack in concentration, tummy aches, blemished skin and weak hair – not even thinking about the possibility that this may be all caused by our nutrition.

YOU ARE WHAT YOU EAT

I love to know why things happen and how they happen. I enjoy understanding why I have stomach cramps or a bloated belly on one day but feel totally fine on another. It's also fascinating to observe how my dad is super-tired one day and the next he's full of energy until late at night – and yes, it depends on what he ate right before. I would just feel uncomfortable living my life without fully understanding it. I enjoy taking matters into my own hands. And that's a crucial point right here: my own hands. Everyone can decide on their own path and I wouldn't want to make decisions for anyone. The long-term motivation for this lifestyle is based on me taking responsibility for my own body, own health and own inner well-being. I took the decision for myself and feel so healthy, energetic and happy with the outcome! What is my best friend doing? That's for her to decide, just like for every other individual out there. But if you want to follow 'my path' towards a healthy life using your own motivation, I'm more than happy to provide help and guidance. That's also why I want to give a general overview on foods at the very beginning of this book.

I WANT MY FOOD TO TASTE GOOD

And I mean really, really good. Thank goodness I realized quickly that it doesn't take extraordinary skills or hours in the kitchen for that. It's less work than you expect. Fresh ingredients, just as nature gave them to us. Unprocessed, uncomplicated and often even cheaper than processed foods, stacked with vitamins, minerals and fibre that keep us healthy and youthful from the inside out. And it's not about 'low carb' or 'low fat' at all. I am not talking about a special diet that leaves you with a growling stomach, or a form of nutrition that requires a substitute for everything. Your food being pure and natural – that's important. That's what 'healthy' means to me. It's about enjoying food, about listening to your body and finding out what keeps you fit and feeling great. This might be somewhat different for you than it is for me. But if you start paying attention to what you are eating, you can crack your own code. That's why this book is suitable for everyone – no matter your age, gender or the weight you are aiming for.

WHERE DOES YOUR FOOD COME FROM?

Do you really need ready meals every day, that were made by some stranger using ingredients (you can't even pronounce) weeks ago, are industrially processed and wrapped in plastic? Maybe it wasn't even a person but a machine. Maybe it tasted like cardboard first and was then spiced up with a lot of sugar, artificial flavours and colours. Have you ever asked yourself why a cut apple goes brown within a couple of days, while a ready meal stays 'fresh' for half a century? I doubt you need ready meals at all. At least you won't once you've realized how quickly you can cook a delicious meal with natural ingredients. And maybe your never-ending cravings will come to an end as well. Because they mostly don't originate from too few calories – we definitely eat enough of those – but from your body's demand to finally get all the nutrients it simply cannot find in ready meals. The quality of foods was better back in the day, fewer chemicals and hormones were used and industrial products weren't processed as much. My grandma has been eating whatever she felt like since day one and ... she's still pretty healthy.

WHEN HEALTHY EATING BECAME IMPORTANT TO ME

I was raised with a healthy style of eating – thanks mum! But it started to be very important to me when I went to the gym at the age of 16. Everybody knows that training won't show results if you don't eat properly. But do I have to consume powder from containers and swallow pills? Is that 'healthy'? I was sceptical. Since then I've been looking deeper into what a body really needs to have enough energy, feel strong and be supplied with all the nutrients it needs. This, as a side note, was also affecting other areas of my life. Besides smaller things like healthy long hair, strong nails and clearer skin, I also started noticing an increase in my performance. I finished school with top grades, I was focussed on doing my job and, most importantly, I approached every day with a positive and balanced attitude. Stress is created by ourselves and, at the end of the day, it's just a matter of personal perception. But that's a topic for another book.

I WANT TO UNDERSTAND MY FOOD

Thanks to my strong connection to fitness and vitality, things like calories, proteins and fibre are important to me. It's not about building a negative and controlling attitude towards food, but rather to embody a way to understand it. To know what it's made of, what your body will do with it and what the effects will be. If you don't feel comfortable with this topic and tend to have an 'abnormal' relationship with food, don't pay any attention to the nutritional information. You do you! What matters most is the quality and naturalness of your food, everything else is secondary.

WHY BOWLS?

Now there's just this last question to be answered. A bowl is a piece of tableware. When dealing with a bowl-dish, the whole meal is served in a single bowl. This trend originates from the United States, but was actually inspired by Buddhism. You are supposed be conscious and aware while eating from a bowl. How many times do we almost rashly devour a meal without noticing what it smells like, tastes like and feels like in the mouth. With a bowl, you can hold it in both hands, perceive the weight of the meal and feel its warmth. A bowl is always one serving – you can immediately tell when the bowl is full. You can't pile up your food sky-high, as we tend to do on a dinner plate. Also the ingredients are not placed apart from each other, but their flavours interact, combine and add up. A bowl is also the perfect dish in which you can serve your food creatively, so that it is pleasing to the eye. Enjoyment is increased, you are left with a nice feeling in your gut, and in the end your digestion will thank you for that.

LOCAL INGREDIENTS

Since I still live in Germany, I can only guarantee that the ingredients I use are available in organic, German supermarkets. It might happen that something specific isn't common in your country. If so: feel free to swap it! No need to skip an entire recipe because of one missing ingredient – it will probably turn out just as good with your local alternative! I also order some packaged food online – the internet has (almost) everything!

And now, please enjoy reading, cooking and getting inspired!

Pamela xx

Food Knowledge

1

Ever since sports and fitness became such major parts of my life, nutrition has become an equally important topic for me as well. I'm always asking myself: what does my body really need in order to have enough energy, feel strong and to be supplied with all the nutrients it needs? I want to know and understand what's in my food and how my body deals with it. To me, it's very eye-opening how the right nutrition can positively impact performance, concentration and mood. That's why conscious eating is not 'only' important for your physical health.

On the following pages I have collected fundamental knowledge that will help you understand what you are actually eating – and what 'healthy' means after all. It does not matter whether you are new to the whole topic of nutrition, or just want to renew your knowledge – everyone should find something to benefit from. I do not claim that the knowledge part is fully 'complete' – you never stop learning anyway when it comes to healthy nutrition. I basically gathered what are, in my opinion, the most important elements. The first step to improving your diet should be a little easier when you understand your food. I'm very positive that this will help you on your journey to take responsibility for your body, soul & wellbeing. I enjoy being in charge of my own life and health, and I hope to pass on this spark to you.

FRUITS

Fruits describe both fruits and seeds that can usually be consumed raw. They generally grow on shrubs, trees and bushes. There are some kinds of vegetables like cucumbers, tomatoes and peppers that, from a botanical viewpoint, are considered fruit because they grow as the result of flowers being pollinated. We can distinguish between tropical fruit, wild, citrus, pip and stone fruits, berries and nuts.

Just like vegetables, fruits contain tons of vitamins, minerals and fibre and generally offer a high concentration of nutrients. In addition, fruits feature higher amounts of fructose and contain fruit acids. In combination with their flavours, those fruit acids are responsible for triggering our digestive juices.

Fruits and vegetables are the most essential sources for one of the most important nutrients: vitamin C. We need this vitamin for our immune system, for our connective tissues and to improve the absorption of iron. The daily requirement of vitamin C is 100mg, which is almost covered by two oranges. Apart from that, vitamin C is primarily found in strawberries, citrus fruits and blackcurrants.

Just as in vegetables, valuable phytochemicals are also found in fruits. Orange-coloured fruits like apricots or papayas, for example, contain the phytochemical beta-carotene. This natural colourant gets converted into vitamin A and is responsible for various important tasks like regulating cell growth and controlling the immune system. Beta-carotene also has strong antioxidant properties and fights free radicals. These radicals are harmful, unstable atoms created naturally in our bodies through oxidation – increasingly due to stress, smoking and simply getting older. In abundance, they are harmful to cells, speed up ageing, promote inflammation and diseases. Antioxidants help us cope with those free radicals and maintain a healthy balance.

When food shopping, you sometimes find fruits that are still quite hard and unripe. That's not a problem when we're talking about those kinds of fruits that continue to ripen after being harvested. For example pears, kiwis, mangos and plums. Make sure not to store these fruits in the fridge as room temperature works better for them. To speed up the ripening process, you can also store them next to apples. Apples release a gas called ethylene, which encourages plants to ripen – a simple but effective lifehack! Generally speaking, local fruits should be stored chilled or cold, exotic kinds prefer to be kept at room temperature.

Apples

support a lot of functions in the body like the gut flora, the lung function and even the brain function thanks to many highly effective secondary plant substances. They can further lower cholesterol levels and prevent cardiovascular problems.

Bananas

regulate the blood pressure with the trace mineral potassium they contain and can therefore prevent heart attacks and arteriosclerosis. Provide energy quickly and are popular with athletes as a snack before and after a workout.

Berries

are mostly very low in sugar. In general they are a rich source of antioxidants and vitamins. Strawberries contain a lot of vitamin C (around 60mg/100g). There's generally no difference in vitamins for frozen berries.

Coconuts

are considered superfoods because of their density of vitamins and minerals. They have antibacterial properties, support digestion, prevent dehydration and are rich in antioxidants.

Dates

have a lot of calories (around 280kcal/100g), but close to no fat and a lot of vitamin C, vitamin B, as well as potassium, iron and calcium. With their natural sweetness, dates are a great substitute for industrial sugar.

Figs

are low in acids and high in fibre, that's how they support digestion and help with constipation. They also belong to the group of the most alkaline foods. Dried figs contain more calcium than milk!

Grapefruit

contain bitter-tasting substances which support fat-burning processes and lower blood sugar levels. This prevents diabetes. Studies have also shown that grapefruit are able to avoid weight gain!

Grapes

contain the secondary plant substance resveratrol which protects the nerves, lowers blood pressure and controls cholesterol levels. Its highest concentration is in the skin of the grape and is produced by the plant as a protection from fungi.

Lemons

stand out with a high vitamin C content (around 50mg/100g), and in this way support the immune system, protecting our cells and preventing food cravings.

Mangos

are rich in beta-carotene, potassium, vitamins A, C and E. Glutamic acid supports our memory by increasing concentration and stimulating nerves.

Oranges & Mandarins

contain lots of vitamins and therefore protect hair and skin. The active substance synephrine lowers the cholesterol level. Eating the whole fruit is better than drinking orange juice!

Peaches

are very low in sugar (around 9g/100g) and the beta-carotene they contain supports eye and skin health. Their enzymes also regulate the metabolism and support digestion.

Pears

are among the fruit with the highest fibre content, with about 3.3g/100g. Calcium and potassium support a good metabolism and help drain excess water retention. They contain fewer fruit acids than apples and are therefore more gentle on our teeth.

Plums

are considered natural laxatives thanks to their water-soluble plant substances. You shouldn't eat too many plums at once or drink too much water while eating them, otherwise the pectin and cellulose will swell up even more and you can end up being bloated.

Pomegranates

are low in calories (around 74kcal/100g), contain the unsaturated fatty acids known as punicic acid and the secondary plant substance punicalagin. These have anti-inflammatory effects and may prevent Alzheimer's disease.

Watermelons

dilate blood vessels with the amino acid L-citrulline and therefore increase blood flow and heart health. The high fructose content can cause bloating, so it is better not eat watermelons at the same time as other foods.

WHERE TO KEEP WHICH FRUITS?

FRIDGE	ROOM TEMPERATURE	DARK AND COOL
Apricots, Figs, Grapes, Kiwis, Plums, Strawberries	Citrus fruits, Tropical fruits (like Bananas, Mangos, Pineapples)	Apples, Pears

QUICK TIP: Seeds from fruit such as grapes also contain valuable nutrients so consider eating the seeds as well! The fact that plants naturally contain seeds is quite self-explanatory, isn't it? Seedless fruits were only created for human consumption, so the ones with seeds are always the more natural and healthy choice!

How much fruit and vegetables should you eat per day? If you ask me, there can never be enough. I'm not 'afraid' of fructose. Generally we speak of a minimum of five servings of vegetables and fruits per day. A serving should fit in your hand and is therefore easy to measure. If you struggle reaching this amount, let me advise you to take advantage of smoothies – green ones are my favourite. Make them with fresh or frozen fruits or vegetables, blended freshly yourself as a drink or smoothie bowl. You can also find several smoothie bowl recipes in this book. Otherwise, you can also change things up a little bit and try frying the fuits briefly in a pan with some cinnamon, combining them with vegetables or enjoying them plain and raw.

Some kinds of fruits like bananas, pineapples or mangos have a naturally high amount of fruit sugar. This sugar is not the same as industrially produced sugar, since a fruit also provides you with a lot of valuable enzymes, fibre, vitamins and minerals, which help your body handle the sugar. Still, fruits can – depending on the level of fructose they contain – heavily influence your blood sugar level. I perceive fruits as the healthy 'sweets' of nature.

INFO: Minerals are firmly fixed in the cells of fruits and vegetables. By blending or puréeing the cells get destroyed, the minerals are suddenly free and easier to absorb during digestion. Homemade juices, smoothies and smoothie bowls take advantage of this.

VEGETABLES

Vegetable is a collective term for the edible parts of plants or whole edible plants. Compared to fruit, which can usually be eaten and harvested from the same plant for years and years, vegetables are mostly harvested just once or maybe twice a year and then need to be re-planted. Vegetables are usually distinguished by which parts of the plant are used, for example leaves, fruits, flowers, tubers, bulbs, sprouts, stalks or roots. You can also include herbs and mushrooms into the family of vegetables. Definitions are not 100% accurate though, if we're being precise, mushrooms are a life form of their own. Some vegetables, like cucumbers, tomatoes or peppers, are actually fruits from a botanical point of view.

As children we learn that vegetables are very healthy. Why is this? When compared to other foods, vegetables have the highest concentration of nutrients. That's why vegetables should be the biggest part of a meal when looking at a healthy and well-balanced diet. The recipes in this book are actually all based on vegetables! It's therefore a great start to integrate one bowl recipe a day into your meal plan. Thanks to a high degree of water – about 75 to 95% – vegetables are also low in calories. This low dose of energy, combined with a high fibre content, means that the daily consumption of vegetables prevents obesity and other diseases. Vegetables are rich in vitamins and minerals, too. Our body cannot produce these itself, so we have to eat them with our food – this means they are 'essential'. The dietary fibre contained in vegetables is only partially digested. These plant fibres absorb harmful substances, encourage our digestion and increase the volume of our gut content. This means they swell up and keep us full for a longer period of time. Further, plant fibres have a positive effect on cholesterol and blood sugar levels. Most people eat too little fibre nowadays. This results in a sluggish, poor digestion and can easily cause constipation, which is rather unpleasant. You should aim to eat at least 30g of fibre on a daily basis, preferably from vegetables, fruits and wholegrain products. The consumption of, for example, an apple results in about 3g fibre, a slice of wholegrain bread equals about 6–7g.

When selecting vegetables and fruits, I make sure to pick a big variety of different colours. The colours of the plants are down to the secondary plant substances they contain. There are 100,000 different ones known to date – and they all have different tasks and functions within the plants.

Avocados

are high in healthy, unsaturated fatty acids. They contribute to a clear skin and keep us full for longer. They also contain a lot of potassium and secondary plant substances.

Beetroots

contain nitrates that lower blood pressure and increase endurance. That's why athletes love them. Beetroots also have anti-oxidative and anti-inflammatory features thanks to their betalains.

Broccoli

contains a lot of vitamins, minerals and secondary plant substances. They also feature kaempferol, which is highly anti-inflammatory and therefore known to prevent various diseases.

Carrots

are known for their high content of beta-carotene, which is the reason for the carrot's orange colour. The human body converts the beta-carotene into vitamin A during digestion. This supports skin health and prevents it from early ageing.

Cucumbers

have detoxifying and moisturizing properties. The enzyme peptidase contributes to a better digestion – just like the dietary fibres that cucumbers are mostly made of. They also contain an extremely high amount of water.

Lentils, Peas & Beans

uncooked and measured dry, these contain more protein than meat and are therefore an important source of protein for vegetarians and vegans. The high fibre, potassium and magnesium content also supports a healthy blood pressure.

Lettuce

consists mostly of water and fibre and has little to no calories. Lamb's lettuce is especially rich in vitamins and minerals. Bitter-tasting substances – found for example in chicory – support digestion and strengthen the immune system.

Mushrooms

mostly contain a lot of protein (e.g. porcini mushrooms about 5.5%) and iron. For example, 100g of chanterelles contain, at about 6.5mg, half of your daily requirement of iron.

Onions & Garlic

both have a high content of sulphur compounds that are antioxidative and responsible for the aroma and tanginess. They also contribute to fat-burning and the regulation of blood pressure.

Peppers

contain lots of vitamins. One red pepper already covers the daily requirement of vitamin C (around 100mg). That helps the immune system, prevents illness and supports the eyes. Carotenoids also contribute to this.

Potatoes & Sweet Potatoes

contain valuable proteins as well as minerals such as potassium. Sweet potatoes contain more fibre, vitamin A and E. On the other hand, 'normal' potatoes are grown in many regions of Europe and are often more affordable.

Radishes

have, thanks to the mustard oil found in them, antibacterial, anti-inflammatory and antibiotic properties and give dishes some tangy spiciness. Studies even link mustard oil with cancer-healing properties.

Spinach

is rich in minerals and essential vitamins. It's low in calories and offers lots of fibre and antioxidants. This is why it supports digestion and prevents ageing. Its super-high iron content is actually a myth. Baby spinach is often eaten raw, just like a salad.

Squash

are antioxidative and support our immune system, which comes in handy during the autumn season. The essential amino acid tryptophan, which is found in the seeds, is a great help during the production of happiness hormones. Pumpkin seed oil supports the bladder and prostate.

Tomatoes

are particularly rich in vitamins C and B, which also supports concentration. One of the most important substances in tomatoes is the phytochemical lycopene. It prevents heart disease and arteriosclerosis.

Zucchini

belong to the family of cucurbits (which also includes squash, melons, cucumbers). They contain magnesium, potassium, folate and a lot of other healthy substances. A small zucchini (or courgette) covers over one-third of the daily requirement of vitamin C!

- When **stewing**, vegetables are cooked with little to barely any added liquid, so mainly in their own juices.

- **Steaming** means that the vegetables are cooked in water vapour, for example with the help of a steamer basket over boiling water.

- When you're cooking vegetables by briefly putting them into boiling water and then immediately refreshing them with ice-cold water, it's called '**blanching**'.

Secondary plant substances are related to the appearance of the plant, its smell or for protection against pests. They are not essential for life, but still have positive effects on our bodies. For example, they can lower the risk of developing various diseases and cholesterol levels, support the blood vessels and even have antibacterial and anti-inflammatory properties attributed to them.

To make sure your vegetables don't always taste the same, you can change things up with seasoning or use different preparation and cooking techniques. When cooking vegetables you should try to keep the heat rather low – otherwise you'll risk destroying vitamins and nutrients. Besides the unpleasant taste, you shouldn't heat green salads at all, since these are very heat-sensitive and would lose all their healthy nutrients. Stewing, steaming and blanching are the least harmful techniques that maintain as many nutrients as possible. When vegetables are treated in a rather delicate way you can get the most positive, healthy effects from them. I also love sautéing vegetables in a pan or roasting them in the oven – the flavours are incredible!

For some types of vegetables it's absolutely necessary to cook them, because they can be harmful to health when consumed raw. For example, potatoes and unripe aubergines contain the natural poison solanine which is toxic to humans in larger quantities but can be reduced when cooking. This is the reason why you should also always cut off any green parts and sprouts on potatoes and avoid eating unripe, still green tomatoes. When on the go, I love having crunchy vegetable sticks made from carrots, peppers and cucumbers with me. I carry them in a stainless-steel container, washed and cut up.

For raw vegetables especially, but also for vegetables in general, I strongly recommend buying organic ones. You can expect a lower pesticide load this way. And as we know, most of the vitamins hide in the skin! So if the skin is edible, I like to eat organic vegetables with the skin on.

If you want to get the most out of your vegetables, you have to pay attention to proper storage. Generally speaking, chilling slows down a plant's metabolism and vegetables therefore stay fresh for longer. Most types of vegetables can be kept in the fridge without any problems, but not every single type is best stored in the cold. Vegetables with, for example, a high water content are sensitive to cool temperatures: they quickly lose their flavour and should therefore not be stored in the fridge. Vegetables and fruit from warm climate zones – for example, avocados or bananas – also don't like it cold. Onions and garlic may go mouldy faster if they are kept in the fridge. As a rule of thumb, the longer you store a vegetable, the more nutrients, vitamins and flavours will be lost. So it's best to plan your grocery shopping wisely.
If you would like to store your vegetables for even longer, you can freeze most kinds. To prepare them it's advisable to wash and blanch the vegetables first. By blanching them, the nutrients, colour and taste stay intact for longer.

QUICK TIP:

Vegetables should always be kept separate from fruit. The reason for this is the ripening gas ethylene, which is emitted by apples, pears, peaches and plums. The gas causes vegetables to ripen, but also to rot more quickly.

STORING AND PRESERVING VEGETABLES: DOS AND DON'TS

FRIDGE	ROOM TEMPERATURE	DARK AND COOL	DON'T FREEZE!
Asparagus, Broccoli, Cabbage, Carrots, Cauliflower, Iceberg Lettuce, Kohlrabi, Lettuce, Mushrooms, Peas, Radishes, Spinach, Spring Onions	Avocados, Beans, Cucumbers, Peppers, Tomatoes, Zucchini	Aubergines, Garlic, Onions, Potatoes, Squash	Artichoke, Beansprouts, Onions Radishes, Vegetables with high water content (Cucumber, Lettuce etc.)

HERBS & SPICES

Spices are mostly made from dried plants or parts of plants like the bark (e.g. cinnamon), roots (e.g. ginger), seeds (e.g. nutmeg) and fruits (e.g. black pepper, vanilla). Herbs are available fresh or dried, and some are also considered to be spices. The reason for their strong taste and smell are the essential oils they contain. These can encourage appetite and digestion, as well as intensify and complement weaker flavours in other foods.

In my opinion, the use of herbs and spices as a refinement for all kinds of dishes is totally underrated in most regions. They just add that certain something to a dish. Moreover they are healthy – herbs have been used in medicine for countless years. Herbs like caraway, marjoram or fennel seeds, for example, increase the body's tolerance for legumes and are used to calm tummy aches and bloating. Parsley prevents bladder and kidney stones, increases the formation of blood and balances the digestion.

Spices are more commonly and generously used in warmer regions. A reason could be that spices help to preserve foods and, due to high humidity, there was a bigger need for that back in the day. Cinnamon, for example, works well against mould; and cloves and garlic can help to tackle E. coli.

You can also plant your own herbs at home – even if you don't have a garden! Try to locate them in a sunny place, for example your kitchen window sill. The following herbs are pretty easy to grow indoors: parsley, mint, basil, oregano, rosemary, coriander and thyme. Apart from cooking, they also work great for teas.

TIP:

Spices and dried herbs should be stored in dark, sealed containers, because they lose their colour and aroma when exposed to light. When cooking with fresh herbs, it's handy to know that the more finely you chop them, the more essential oils you release. Use the herbs as quickly as possible after chopping them so that the essential oils don't evaporate.

INFO:

Strictly speaking, salt is a mineral and not a spice. It's essential to life but often put in a negative context in relation to water retention. Beware: not all salts are created equal! In industrially made products you will often find cheap iodized salt or table salt. They are missing minerals that our bodies need to process salt correctly. That's the reason people say there's no need to be afraid of using genuine sea salt or Himalayan salt. Those aren't connected to water retention or other negative side effects.

GRAINS & PSEUDO-GRAINS

Grains is a collective term for so-called sweet grasses, whose seeds we use for food. These grains are also called cereals. Corn, wheat and rice are the most commonly farmed grains and play a major role in feeding the world's population. They belong to the oldest known foods. Grains are used to produce bread, muesli, coffee, beer and other alcoholic drinks as well as animal feed.

Grains mostly consist of starch and have an overall high nutritional value. They are rich in fibre, carbohydrates, vitamins and calcium. To make the best use out of these valuable nutrients I recommend consuming fresh wholegrain products. When making wholegrain flour, the husks and sprouts are also ground up and included in the final product, which is totally different from the commonly used wheat flour type 405 (the standard white flour). For example, the outer layers of the grains contain protein, magnesium, vitamin B1 and fibre.

If you own a high-power blender, you can grind your own whole-grain flour freshly at home. Alternatively, some organic supermarkets – at least in Germany, it might differ from country to country – offer the use of grist mills in the store, so you can grind your own flour when buying a pack of whole grains. My mum used to do that every time she baked bread but last Christmas we finally got her (or us) a grist mill for our kitchen.

Over the years, grains have been altered and manipulated through breeding and hybridization by humankind. The goal was to make crops resistant to pests and environmental factors and increase the yield by growing bigger seeds. In the baking process, less time-consuming processes are now being used as well. More and more people have an allergic or sensitive reaction when consuming food containing gluten. For those people, pseudo-grain crops are a true alternative. Pseudo-grains are the seeds of plants that are not considered to be sweet grasses. These include amaranth, quinoa, buckwheat and hemp. They resemble grains in appearance and have valuable ingredients but do not contain any gluten. This also means that you are not able to bake a loaf of bread just using those seeds on their own. But other than for baking bread, they work great for a lot of recipes!

Buckwheat

is a pseudo-cereal and 100g contains around 10g of protein that's very well absorbed by the body. Buckwheat can prevent diabetes and effect blood sugar levels positively.

Corn

has its origins in Mexico and we can cover about 34% of our daily requirements of magnesium with 100g corn. It's also gluten-free.

Oats

have a great nutritional balance and the highest values in vitamin B_1 (590μg/100g) and B_6 (160μg/100g) out of all grains. Special dietary fibres prevent an increase of blood sugar and cholesterol levels and keep you full for a long time.

Quinoa

is a real superfood: it contains more minerals than the usual grains, e.g. 8mg of iron in 100g quinoa – that's almost twice what wheat offers. It also contains valuable proteins (around 14g/100g) with all the essential amino acids.

Rice

exists in more than 100,000 different varieties. Brown rice is also a great source of magnesium, which is beneficial for stress relief. Unfortunately rice is often contaminated with the toxin arsenic, which is reduced when you rinse it thoroughly before cooking.

Rye

is rich in the protein building block lysin, that promotes the formation of new blood vessels. Thanks to its high fibre content, rye keeps us full and is beneficial for both blood sugar and cholesterol levels.

Spelt

is mostly easy digestible for people suffering from food allergies, has a slight nutty flavour and has more vitamins and minerals than wheat does. The silicic acid it contains is beneficial to skin, hair and nails.

Wheat

is most commonly known as the basis for white bread, which consists of simple – also called 'empty' – carbohydrates. They have a negative impact on blood sugar levels. Besides the common white flour, wholegrain flour is also available.

LEGUMES

Legumes are plants and seeds that ripen inside pods. The most commonly known are beans, peas, chickpeas, lentils, soy and lupines. From a botanical viewpoint, peanuts are legumes as well. When measured dry, legumes contain more protein than meat or any other plant-based food, which makes them especially important for vegetarians and vegans as a source of protein. The proteins are of a high biological value but – if consumed on their own – don't contain all the amino acids (see page 50, Proteins). Above all, they are great at keeping us full and satisfied for a long time, as they contain up to an incredible 20% fibre. Please note, all percentages refer to dry, uncooked beans. The high fibre content results in slower digestion and keeps blood sugar levels constant. Minerals like iron, potassium and magnesium found in legumes have a positive effect on our health, too.

Legumes are not just limited to side dishes but can also be used to make soups, purées and spreads. Further you can process them into flour or even noodles. Besides protein, carbohydrate and fibre, legumes consist of less than 1g of fat per 100g. An exception to this are soy beans which have 5g of fat. Soybeans can be processed to make the popular soy milk and also oil, flour, sauce, paste, tofu, tempeh or other meat substitutes. Thanks to their diversity they are one of the most commonly used legumes. However, I have not used any soy products in this cookbook as I see plenty of reasons not to consume them on a regular basis: about 80% of all soybeans worldwide are processed into cheap animal feed. This requires enormous amounts of farmland and unfortunately forests have to be cleared to achieve this. Also 80% of the soybeans available worldwide are genetically modified. They also contain plant oestrogens, so-called isoflavones, which bind to our hormone receptors and can mess up our hormonal balance.

GOOD TO KNOW

Do not eat legumes uncooked, as they contain harmful and even partially toxic substances that are only neutralized by cooking. To improve the digestion of legumes, you can either let the dried ones soak in water before cooking, or even let them sprout. The longer you soak them the better. This reduces the time needed for cooking, minerals can be absorbed more effectively and the legumes become easier on the stomach as the non-digestible carbohydrates dissolve. Lentils and hulled peas can be cooked directly without prior soaking. In general, hulled legumes are even easier to digest. Before soaking you should rinse your dried legumes thoroughly in a sieve under running water. Then, place them in a saucepan or bowl and add three times the amount of water. Cover with a lid or towel and let them soak for about 12 hours, or overnight, at room temperature. When done, pour away the water from soaking as it contains the dissolved indigestible carbohydrates that we wanted to get rid of in the first place. Rinse the legumes once again under running water and then cook according to the instructions. Cooked or canned chickpeas can be shelled before using them, and this makes the dishes creamier and finer. To do so, rub the chickpeas between your hands in a bowl full of water. The shells will float to the top and can simply be skimmed off.

I always have legumes like peas, chickpeas and red lentils in my cupboard, as well as rice and the pseudo-grain quinoa.

FISH

Fish is a traditional source of protein in the human diet. Until now, around 17% of our protein requirement on average is supplied by fish, and this proportion is increasing. Fish offers lots of valuable ingredients including, for example, the protein building block tryptophan, which forms the 'happiness' hormone serotonin and may prevent cardiovascular disease. Furthermore, fish is especially known for its omega-3 fatty acid content. These guard against diseases like heart attacks and high blood pressure. Although fish itself is very healthy, its quality may vary nowadays and consumption can lead to some serious problems.

Experts warn of an ever-increasing pollution from microplastics and heavy metals like mercury. Fish higher in the food chain experience a higher toxic load. When having a look on a sushi menu, you will think that 90% are made with salmon, prawns or tuna. These became trendy quite a while ago – and not without consequences. Thanks to the immense requirement for these species in particular, oceans are overfished mercilessly. According to the Living Planet Report 2018 by the World Wide Fund for Nature (WWF) the population of fish and marine life in general has been cut in half over the last 40 years. Our oceans do offer various other species and creatures though, which are not yet as well known or as 'sexy', like herring, clam, seaweed or algae. Due to overfishing and increasing demand, fish are also being farmed in so-called aquacultures. At first glance, this appears to be a good solution. But unfortunately it has flaws. Because, as in large-scale livestock farming on land, the fish have to live in tight spaces, which causes diseases to spread quickly. In several countries medicines like antibiotics are added to the fish feed. To make space for fish farms, large forest areas are cleared as well. Most of the farmed species are carnivores (such as tuna and salmon) so their feed still has to be caught in the ocean. This, in return, further promotes overfishing. There's an alternative, called 'integrated multi-trophic aquaculture' which is dedicated to using environmentally friendly ways of farming. And on a final note, the fishing industry is responsible for over one million tonnes of plastic pollution in our oceans.

For me, the flavour of fish isn't a must. Because of this, and the problems stated above, I have decided to consume no or close to no more fish at all. So I'd like to emphasize and advise you: if you are buying fish, look out for sustainably caught products or organic fish. And please don't go for the popular species too often.

MEAT

Meat can be taken from animals that are bred for slaughter, such as beef, pork, lamb, goat, chicken and turkey, or from wild hunted species such as deer and wild boar. In other countries or cultural areas, animals like bison, buffalo or reindeer are also consumed. Meat offers a high protein content (for example turkey has around 23g/100g), which is, just like the iron it contains, very high in bioavailability. That means it can be easily absorbed and processed in our body when eaten. Further, meat contains vitamins (A, B, D and others) and minerals like sodium, zinc and potassium.

In recent years in particular, the consumption of meat is being discussed more and more and we should all be aware of the problems factory farming introduce. By now, scientists have also proved a direct link between meat consumption in industrial countries and climate change. This makes sense, as livestock farming produces more emissions than cars, ships and air travel together! Also the high demand for soy as a feed results in increased emissions of greenhouse gases. The clearing of rainforests to make space for grazing land or soy plantations is also a direct consequence.

I don't exclusively follow a vegetarian or vegan diet. But I also don't reject styles of eating that don't incorporate animal products. I try to consciously live off plant-based foods for the most part, and am well aware of the consequences frequent meat consumption brings.

If I decide to buy meat I only go for unprocessed and premium, organic quality. So I'd rather have a piece of pure chicken breast than a processed sausage or salami. Further, the animals should have enough free space in the fields, only be fed with organic food and not be pumped full of drugs. No doubt this meat does cost more but I think quality has its price, so you shouldn't be stingy here. Also, the high price may be a reason to perceive meat as a special treat again, like a 'Sunday roast', not as an everyday necessity.

From my personal experience it takes a while until you feel like a meal is 'complete' without any meat or fish. Until a year ago, this was also still the case for me, but luckily it has changed since then. A meal consisting of only vegetables, grains and fruits can be 'complete' as well. But you have to allow this process for some time. With creativity and delicious recipes, you will not miss the daily consumption of meat – I promise.

MILK & ALTERNATIVES

Milk is sourced from previously pregnant mammals. In Europe this usually refers to cows' milk, if not stated otherwise. The milk is processed and divided into the following kinds: raw milk (unprocessed and fresh), whole milk (at least 3.5% fat), semi-skimmed milk (1.5–1.8% fat) and skimmed milk (maximum of 0.3% fat). Sales of raw milk are limited in England, Wales and Northern Ireland, and it is illegal to distribute it in Scotland. Cow's milk contains about 87% water and provides not only lactoprotein, fat and carbs, but also essential amino acids, vitamins and minerals as well as calcium (around 120mg/100g). Milk is also the basis for other foods like cheese, yoghurt, cream and butter, which are produced in dairy factories. In Europe, a single person consumes on average about 90kg of milk and dairy products per year.

A cow can provide up to 50 litres of milk every day. This is the result of years of breeding, since cows were originally only able to provide 10 litres of milk a day. Here you can see the impact of industrialization in dairy production, always aiming for the highest output as possible. Cows are often kept in large herds and are given concentrated feed rather than fresh grass. To be able to produce milk, cows need to give birth to calves which are taken from them afterwards. Only a few months later the cows are artificially inseminated and are therefore almost pregnant non-stop. After four or five years they are slaughtered.

Alternatives to cow's milk are plant-based drinks, which are based on water. These are not as rich in nutrients, but are dairy and lacto-protein free. In the United States the sales of plant-based milk substitutes, such as almond milk, increased by 80% over the last six years, meanwhile animal milk sales dropped by 20% over the same period.

I have not consumed milk, and only a minimum of dairy products, for a long time now. That's why you can barely find them in my recipes. In my opinion a mother cow's milk is designed for her calves and the hormones it contains are not supposed to get into our human bodies. Moreover, the plant-based milk tastes way better to me, and there are already great substitutes for dairy products like cheese, yoghurt and cream.

TIP:

Make your own plant milk: soak 50–100g grain (e.g. oats) or nuts (e.g. almonds) overnight in lukewarm water. Then, blend with 1 litre of fresh water using a high-power blender. Pour the mixture in a nut milk or linen bag and wring out. Store the milk in the fridge.

Almond milk

is probably the most common nut milk. Slight marzipan flavour but all in all neutral and therefore very versatile.

Coconut milk

is available in a creamy, thick version with a high fat content (14–20%) and as a lighter, fat-free coconut drink. Has a nutty, exotic flavour.

Hazelnut milk

thanks to its nutty taste this is fantastic when used to make a mug of hot chocolate. It's not as commonly found in supermarkets yet.

Hemp milk

is made from peeled hemp seeds (pseudo-cereal). A 500ml serving contains the daily recommended dietary requirement of omega-3 fatty acids.

Oat milk

has a sweetish taste and is great for cooking and baking. My favourite choice for porridge! Can contain gluten.

Rice milk

tastes very sweet and is gluten-free. That's why it's great for people suffering from allergies and coeliac disease. Recipes that need a little sweetness can be improved without adding sugar.

Soy milk

is rather nutty in taste and well suited to savoury dishes. Since I never use any soy products, soy milk is not found in my recipes.

Spelt milk

has an intense cereal flavour. Fits well with breakfast dishes like muesli or porridge. Contains gluten.

FATS & OILS

Even though some people might think of something bad when hearing 'fats and oils', fat does not make you 'fat' and is not necessarily unhealthy. There are some quite good fats and even ones that are essential for life. For example, our brains consist of 60% fat (referring to its dry weight) and are dependent on high-quality fatty acids. Fats carry not only flavours and taste, but also provide us with energy and are needed for the growth of healthy cells in our bodies. Vitamin A, D, E and K can only be absorbed with the help of fats as well.

Depending on how they are structured, fats can be saturated, monounsaturated or polyunsaturated. To understand these differences, it's handy to imagine their chemical structure. Saturated fatty acids have a hydrogen atom attached to every carbon atom, so they are 'saturated' with hydrogen. Their structure is stable and they are more heat-resistant than other fats. The more saturated a fatty acid is, the more stable and sturdier its shape. These kinds of fats are mostly found in animal fats and have a bad reputation as they can increase cholesterol levels. Unsaturated fatty acids have fewer hydrogen atoms, and are therefore more fragile and more fluid. We divide these between monounsaturated and polyunsaturated fatty acids. Monounsaturated fatty acids strengthen our immune system and are most commonly found in plant-based, healthy foods like almonds, avocados and olives. Polyunsaturated fatty acids cannot be made by our bodies, that's why eating these essential fats with our food is so incredibly important. They are the building blocks of our cells, form immune substances and can be divided in omega-3 and omega-6 fatty acids. The right balance between the two plays an important role. This balance should be at a maximum of 5:1 from omega-6 to omega-3. In western countries the share of omega-6 fatty acids is way too high and we are – with an incredible proportion of 20:1 – far from the optimum. This can have negative effects on our health as too much of omega-6 fatty acids may cause blood clots, inflammation and therefore various illnesses. Omega-3 fatty acids, on the other hand, prevent these effects and guard against heart disease and thrombosis. Great sources for omega-3 fatty acids are flaxseeds, chia seeds, walnuts and algae.

TIP:
Two things happen when heating up some kinds of oils or fats to very high temperatures. On the one hand positive substances are destroyed, and on the other hand dangerous substances like trans fats are created. That's why your best choices for pan-frying, and any other hot cooking technique, are avocado oil, coconut oil and ghee.

Avocado oil

like olive oil, it has a comparably high content of monounsaturated fatty acids and can be heated to unusually high temperatures. Its smoke point is reached at around 250°C.

Coconut oil

has a high content of saturated fats (about 92%) and can therefore be used for cooking at high temperatures. There is no need for coconut oil to undergo heavy processing during production to ensure a long shelf life.

Ghee (clarified butter)

originates from the Ayurvedic cuisine and is clarified butter. It consists of about 68% saturated fatty acids and can be heated up to very high temperatures. It contains 2% each of both omega-6 and omega-3 fatty acids.

Flax oil

is an important source of omega-3 fatty acids (about 56%) and has anti-inflammatory properties. It should be stored in a cool, dark place. I often use flaxseeds in my recipes as I am so convinced of their effect. Do not heat the oil!

Olive oil

contains antioxidants and polyphenols. It mostly consists of mono-unsaturated fats (about 70%). The balance between omega-6 to omega-3 fatty acids is around 8:1 and not entirely optimal. Still, it's known as very healthy for its high amount of oleic acid.

Rapeseed oil

has usually been heavily processed. But there are also extra virgin and cold-pressed ones! The balance between omega-6 to omega-3 fatty acids is 2:1.

Sesame oil

contains around 44% linoleic acid, a poly-unsaturated fatty acid – and the most important omega-6 fatty acid. It also lowers high cholesterol levels and high blood pressure.

Sunflower oil

is a commonly available oil which is highly processed and found in lots of foods as a cheaper alternative to high-quality oils. Contains a very high proportion of omega-6 fatty acids. The ratio to omega-3 fatty acids is 120:1 and therefore extremely bad. That's why I don't use it.

NUTS, SEEDS & KERNELS

Nuts, seeds and kernels are so small but packed with lots and lots of valuable nutrients! I love them and have even called my second Instagram account *pamgoesnuts*, as I am so crazy about them and always have some with me. And they not only taste great – they are also super-healthy. They help to improve concentration and focus. Eating a handful of nuts and seeds a day can help reduce inflammation in our body and therefore prevent illnesses and diseases, positively impact heart health and lower cholesterol levels.

Some people are wary of nuts as they are high in fat and calories. And, of course, a handful of nuts has more calories than a handful of tomatoes. But the fatty acids in nuts are mostly unsaturated and very healthy. Our body needs the omega-3 fatty acids to regulate the immune system and cell growth. Nuts are also rich in omega-6 fatty acids though, which is why you shouldn't eat more than a handful a day.

Studies have also shown that nuts can help people to lose weight! The reason is the high density of nutrients like proteins and fibre that keep you full and satiated for a long period of time. This prevents cravings, you don't overeat as quickly, are less hungry and eat fewer calories in total.

For your everyday nut consumption, focus on nuts that are natural and untreated. Through roasting, valuable fatty acids, antioxidants and vitamins can be lost. When they are industrially processed, unhealthy cheap fats are usually added as well. Salted or spiced nuts can also contain vast amounts of table salt. By the way, most of the antioxidants are located in the skin, so you should always eat them with the skin if possible.

Seeds and kernels also contain valuable ingredients. They contain minerals, vitamins and fibre. Most importantly, seeds offer a good ratio in omega-6 to omega-3 fatty acids. Flaxseeds for example have a ratio of 1:4 which makes them the best plant-based source for omega-3 fatty acids. Two teaspoons of crushed flaxseeds already cover the daily requirement. That's why they became my favourite seeds and are often used in my recipes. Seeds and kernels can be integrated into our diet in many ways. For example as a topping on salads, breads and smoothie bowls, cakes and pies, in oils or plain as a snack.

Almonds

contain large amounts of vitamin E, which is very important for our skin, hair and nails. Almonds also protect against diabetes, Alzheimer's disease and inflammation.

Cashew nuts

compared to other nuts, have a relatively low fat content (about 45g/100g). They contain a lot of magnesium (about 258mg /100g) and are also used as alternatives for dairy products.

Flaxseeds

are locally grown in Europe, Russia or Canada. They are a cheaper alternative to chia seeds. To make it easier to absorb all nutrients you should use crushed and soaked flaxseeds. They are the best plant-based source for omega-3 fatty acids, with a ratio of 1:4.

Hazelnuts

have a high content in lecithin and support nerve and brain function. I love using them as they remind me of the familiar chocolate-nut flavour. They also contain the healthy oleic acid.

Hemp seeds

offer the optimal ratio of omega-6 to omega-3 fatty acids of 3:1 and are therefore a great way to positively influence our daily balance. This also gives them anti-inflammatory properties.

Peanuts

are strictly speaking legumes and contain a lot of protein (about 29g /100g). In my recipes I like using peanut butter for extra protein. When forming complete plant-based proteins, legumes go well with grains. Oatmeal + peanut butter!

Pumpkin seeds

contain a lot of zinc. About 50g of pumpkin seeds contain half of the daily requirement for an adult. Zinc is needed for the immune system and supports healthy skin. They also vitalize the bladder and prostate.

Walnuts

have the highest amount of omega-3 fatty acids (about 10g/100g) and contain a special form of Vitamin E. The amino acid L-arginine can help to reduce high blood pressure.

SUPERFOODS

You can barely imagine Instagram, magazines or supermarkets without superfoods anymore. But still, there is no universal definition for this term. Usually we mean very nutritious foods that have outstanding amounts of vitamins, minerals and antioxidants. They are called 'superfoods' because they feature a concentration of nutrients that is much higher than those of common foods.

It's mostly exotic ingredients that become trendy, like goji berries or chia seeds. What a lot of people do not know is that there are domestic superfoods, like flaxseeds, in Europe. Sustainability is very dear to my heart and that's why I usually go for flaxseeds rather than chia seeds, since their nutritional benefits are quite similar. Exotic superfoods have usually travelled a long way around the globe. This has a negative effect on the price, the nutrient content and the climate. There have also been reports on pesticide-contaminated superfoods from abroad. There's nothing bad about buying exotic superfoods occasionally. But if there is a local alternative, you don't need to consume the imported version in large quantities on a daily basis, do you? That's why you can find a domestic alternative in the list of exotic superfoods – assuming you're based in Europe.

My favourite superfood is the açaí berry. It's from south America and contains over 100,000 antioxidants. That's why it's outstandingly effective against free radicals. Alternatively you can find locally grown blueberries, blackberries or sour cherries in the shops. But I admit they don't come close to the amount antioxidants found in the açaí berry.

Anyone who regularly consumes local superfoods is doing something good for both themselves and the environment. They have antioxidative and anti-inflammatory effects and support detoxification. You shouldn't substitute fruits and vegetables with superfoods, but rather use them to complete your nutrient intake. There is not a single food in the world that is able to cover all the daily requirements of every nutrient, vital substance and mineral anyway. Superfoods are said to be able to prevent diseases like diabetes and vascular diseases as well as boost overall health, but there is no clear scientific evidence available yet. Superfoods unfold their powers in the best way when you combine them with fresh unprocessed foods and a healthy lifestyle. In the end we can all incorporate superfoods to enhance a balanced healthy diet and to add variety on our plates or bowls. Because, yes, they usually taste amazing!

Algae

like chlorella or spirulina stand out due to their high concentration of fibre, antioxidants, iodine and protein. They contain all the essential amino acids, detoxify, have antioxidative effects, and nourish and strengthen the immune system.

Chia seeds

contain more protein than most kinds of grains (minimum 16g/100g). Additionally, they're rich in polyunsaturated fatty acids like omega-3. A locally grown alternative in Europe are flaxseeds (see page 38 – Nuts, Seeds & Kernels).

Cocoa beans

contain the whole spectrum of antioxidants, magnesium and good fats. They brighten the mood, work against depression, tame hunger attacks and have a chocolatey flavour (without the sweetness, since they contain almost no sugar).

Ginger

can reduce the multiplication of viruses, has antibacterial properties, and therefore supports the body, especially when you have a cold. Also popular for the treatment of nausea.

Goji berries

contain essential amino acids that support muscle growth, are rich in antioxidants and vitamin C (up to 150mg/100g). For a European alternative, blackcurrants contain about 177mg/100g of vitamin C.

Hemp seeds

grow on the hemp plant and feature none of the intoxicating substance THC. They are rich in magnesium and iron. They contain 30% protein, all essential amino acids and have an optimal ratio of omega-6 to omega-3 fatty acids.

Matcha

is a green tea available as a powder and contains just about as much caffeine as an espresso, wakes you up and stimulates the central nervous system. The amino acid L-theanine increases both relaxation and concentration.

Turmeric

works as an anti-inflammatory and is used in Ayurvedic medicine as a medical plant. Black pepper and a fatty food help us to absorb the curcumin found in turmeric.

SUGAR & ALTERNATIVES

Sugar consists of crystals and is the product of plants like sugar beets, sugar cane or sugar palms. This always refers to table sugar (saccharose) which consists of half fruit sugar (fructose) and half grape sugar (glucose).

Fructose is sweeter than glucose and is found in large quantities in fruits, which is where it gets its name from. The naming is actually quite confusing because glucose can also be found in fruit. That's why I prefer to speak of fructose and glucose rather than fruit sugar and grape sugar. Glucose is a so-called simple sugar that's absorbed by the body quickly and is considered a simple carbohydrate. It is also naturally extracted in our body by splitting carbohydrates. Glucose and fructose are handled differently inside our bodies. Glucose is absorbed by the liver, depending on its current energy needs, and then sent out to the remaining body cells, as an energy source. When fructose reaches the liver, it is immediately and completely soaked up. The excess energy that isn't needed at that moment – for activities such as movement or concentration – gets stored in the form of fat cells. When you constantly and excessively consume sugar you increase the risk of developing a fatty liver. Sugar also increases the insulin level for some time, which stops the process of fat burning in exactly this period. Furthermore, cells with excess fat start to react poorly to insulin, which forces our body to release more and more of this hormone to make up for it. These high insulin levels can lead to diabetes.

INDUSTRIAL SUGAR AND ITS EMPTY CALORIES

Artificially produced table sugars do not provide any nutrients, but lots and lots of calories instead, which I like to call 'empty' calories as they don't offer any vitamins or minerals and displace other nutritious foods from our daily diet. Yes, your body does need sugar – but it isn't dependent on industrially produced sugar. It can extract the majority of the glucose it needs from foods like rice, oats, vegetables and fruits. You also don't need to be scared of the sugar that is naturally contained in fruit. It's attached to fibre and will therefore only be extracted slowly into the bloodstream. So your liver is not getting flooded by sugars in a short period of time. With sugar, the *speed* of it entering the bloodstream is crucial.

A comparison with alcohol can help to clarify this: if you're drinking alcohol slowly over the course of an entire evening, you can usually cope with the alcohol quite well. If you drink the same amount all at once, you'll end up being drunk in no time.

Further, fruits contain a lot of water. You'd have to eat huge amounts to get to the sugar level of sweets or soft drinks. It's much harder to eat several kilograms of apples or grapes than to drink 1 or 2 litres of soft drinks or fruit juice.

WATCH OUT!

I advise caution with soft drinks, ready meals and energy drinks, and even 'light' products (often with added sweeteners) and fruit juices. One glass of freshly pressed orange juice (250ml) contains around 25g of sugar that quickly enters the blood, without getting stopped. A liquid is basically 'pre-digested' and there is not much left for the body to do. That's why you should eat your fruits rather than drink them.

Studies warn about the health risks that result from excessive sugar consumption, like diabetes and obesity. Today, sugar is found in almost everything! It's quite often added by the food industry to make its products more delicious and to increase the 'addictive potential'. If you take a closer look at the ingredients list, you may notice there's sugar hidden in products you wouldn't even expect to find it in. It's not made easy for us as consumers, as the food industry also uses other names for sugars – like glucose, fructose, dextrose or maltose. Sugar is hidden in, for example, tangy spreads, organic tomato sauces, natural yoghurt and pretzel sticks. This way starters and main courses suddenly become desserts.

Sweeteners like aspartame or sugar substitutes like xylitol, sorbitol or erythritol are sweet, low calorie and commonly used. They can have negative effects on digestion though. I also distance myself from these sugar alternatives because they are generally very artificial. Whenever I want to give my dishes some sweetness I choose the natural sweeteners listed below, as well as whole fruits like bananas or dates. Many consider the 'glycaemic index' – a scale used to determine the effect of carbohydrates on the blood sugar level – as informative and important. The higher the number, the quicker the food raises the blood sugar level – and the quicker it rises, the worse it is.

GOOD TO KNOW

For me, when it comes to sugar, it's about volume. It's totally okay to have sweets once in a while. But it's completely unnecessary to put ourselves through all the added sugars in starters and main dishes. If you want to eat just a little or no industrially made sugar at all, it's normal to go through some kind of detox phase in the beginning. It's common to experience cravings since your body is used to the sugar. I know from my own experience that it's totally possible to adapt to a diet without artificial sugar though, even long-term. Normal sweets will suddenly start to taste way too sweet and 'fake'. Which is good. Because as soon as this happens, you'll notice that you don't miss them anymore.

Agave syrup

is made from the agave plant, is a syrup and easily soluble. Its strong sweetness (about 68% sugar) comes from its extremely high fructose content. But that's also the reason you should not consume it in large quantities – for the sake of your liver – even though its glycaemic index is 'only' around 15.

Coconut blossom sugar

is made from the flowers of the coconut palm and offers a caramel-like flavour. Coconut blossom sugar is, for a kind of sugar, high in nutrients (magnesium, zinc, iron, potassium and others), low in fructose (2–9%) and has a low glycaemic index of about 35. Highly recommended!

Date syrup

has been known as a sweetener for centuries. Studies have shown that natural date syrup works like an antibiotic and may reduce bacterial growth. You can make it yourself by puréeing dates in a high-power blender, perhaps adding a dash of water.

Dried fruits

are made by dehydrating fruits. They lose around 80% of their water content during this process. What's left is mainly fibre and 70% carbohydrates in the form of fructose. This makes dried fruits a sugar bomb when compared to fresh, but they are still healthier than table sugar. Always go for natural, unsulfured dried fruits.

Honey

is the oldest sweetener. It has antibacterial effects and should not be heated over 40°C (so let your tea cool down before adding it), otherwise the good substances will be lost and even a carcinogenic effect can be created! Honey has a sugar content of 80% and its glycaemic index is around 55.

Maple syrup

is the concentrated juice of the Canadian maple tree, which consists of 45% water. It does contain more minerals than table sugar, but not in relevant quantities and that's why you should only consume it in moderation.

NUTRITION TIPS

My rules

Over the last couple of years I have collected more and more knowledge about nutrition and tried out a lot of things. In doing so, I have developed a feeling for what's good for my body and which foods and ways of eating are the best to make me feel fit and comfortable in my own skin. I have gathered these 'rules' on the following two pages. Of course, everyone should find and develop their personal guide in order to be happy with their own nutrition in the long run!

◆ **SIMPLE.** It does not require complicated methods of preparation or exotic ingredients on a daily basis.

◆ **FRESH.** The fresher the ingredients, the more nutrients they have. They also taste better! Food that is locally grown and currently in season is most likely very fresh.

◆ **QUICK.** When you're hungry, you don't want to spend hours in the kitchen. Only a few recipes take a little longer to prepare, bake or cook.

◆ **ECONOMICAL.** For my recipes you don't need a lot of special equipment and most of the ingredients are pretty affordable.

◆ **CREATIVE.** You eat with your eyes first! Starting off with healthy nutrition, it makes sense to dress your dishes beautifully, so you have fun eating. Bowls especially offer a lot of room to be creative!

◆ **PATIENCE.** A dietary change can be a challenge. It may help to start off with little steps. You never stop learning and the deeper you dive into certain topics, the bigger your passion for them will grow.

◆ **NATURAL.** Always buy foods in the most natural form available. So no heavily processed foods, with added sugars, preservatives, etc.

◆ **BALANCE.** Everything in moderation, nothing in excess. Even 3kg of broccoli is unhealthy in the long run.

◆ **HEALTHY IS NOT ALWAYS HEALTHY.** Some digest raw foods well, some get bloated. Some can process gluten and meat well, some don't. It helps to listen to your body to figure out what really makes you feel well.

◆ **THE RIGHT MOTIVATION.** You should improve your diet for yourself, for your body and your own health, even if your friends and family don't want to join you – it's not about the others!

◆ **SUSTAINABLE.** You should always be aware of the consequences that your nutrition might bring. Particularly concerning the consumption of animal products (see pages 32–35, Meat, Fish, Milk).

◆ **KNOWLEDGE.** Let me tell you, the more knowledge I gather, the more I enjoy healthy eating. Once you really understand what's 'good', you automatically lose interest in the 'bad'. Knowledge is power. On top of that, being convinced by the positive effects certain food could or will have in your body, will most likely increase the result. The brain and the power of thoughts are amazing!

◆ **FASTING.** I want to keep this point optional, but I personally feel very well when just eating for a period of 8 hours a day. For example: I feel super-energetic, I am rarely tired and I can concentrate very well. My blood sugar level stays steady for a long time. Further, my digestion is also better balanced. This way of eating is called intermittent fasting. There are also extended fasting cures – for example for a couple of days – that should give your body time and rest to heal itself.

◆ **BODY AWARENESS.** Do you listen to your body? Do you actually realize what causes stomach cramps, headaches or what makes you feel worn out? Do you eat when you're hungry or do you get into a sugar rush? For me it's a great help to observe my body and its condition from a certain distance and to realize what causes which reaction.

◆ **HOMEMADE.** In my everyday life I ALWAYS prefer cooking my own food. You are what you eat. That's why I like to know which ingredients went into my food and if they were good quality. But don't worry, for my recipes you don't need to be a master chef.

◆ **ROUTINE.** If you do something for a long time period, you allow it to become a habit. It will start to be normal and, if you skip it for a day or two, you'll feel like something is missing in your life. I feel this way about little rituals like oil pulling in the morning, my apple cider vinegar shot and also regarding bigger topics like working out regularly, stretching and healthy eating in general.

INFO: OIL PULLING

Before brushing my teeth in the morning, I swirl 1 tsp. of coconut, sesame or olive oil in my mouth, swish it around for 15–30 minutes and then spit it out into the bin. Afterwards, I brush my teeth as usual. This ritual binds toxins, benefits overall oral health, reduces inflammations of the gums and even whitens the teeth!

ANTIOXIDANTS –

to tackle inflammations

On the pages about fruits, nuts, superfoods, fats and oils I have written quite a bit about antioxidants and anti-inflammatory foods. As the topic of inflammations is dear to my heart, I'd like to share some more information on this page.

Antioxidants help us to deal with harmful environmental influences. They are a protective shield of some sort which stops destructive molecules – so-called free radicals. Those free radicals harm our cells, which then weakens the immune system, makes our skin age faster and are associated with diseases like cancer, rheumatism and Alzheimer's disease. Antioxidants minimize the oxidative damage to the cells and therefore have a natural anti-ageing effect from within. Also, they are considered anti-inflammatory – inflammations are known to be the origin of many illnesses. Chronic inflammations in the body promotes asthma, arthritis, diabetes, cardiovascular disease, high blood pressure, Parkinson's and the already mentioned Alzheimer's disease and cancer. An inflammation is the body's own defence mechanism against free radicals, viruses and bacteria. In the long run, an unhealthy diet can cause inflammation as well, since you don't get enough minerals and vitamins and end up being too acidic. The pH value indicates if a liquid is acid or alkaline. Some foods turn alkaline when digested, others are acidic. Let's say we are consuming too many acidifying foods like animal products, milk, sugar, white flour, wheat and alcohol – this results in too much stress for our organs as they are constantly trying to keep the pH value level. But even an unhealthy lifestyle full of stress, negative emotions and smoking can support over-acidification. So this does not mean we should fanatically avoid all these foods – the mantra 'balance is key' applies here as well.

WHAT I CONSIDER INTERESTING

New research shows that obesity is often accompanied by an inflammation of the brain. Therefore, the brain can't process and interpret the body's signal of satiety and the obesity increases steadily. If the inflammation is then decreased (for example by regularly consuming omega-3 fatty acids) the brain will be able to interpret the signals again, which in return helps with weight loss by re-recognizing hunger and the feeling of having had enough.

PROTEINS –

important building blocks for muscles

A protein is a macronutrient and considered to be one of the most important nutrients, along with fat and carbohydrates. A distinction is made between animal- and plant-based proteins. Proteins are an important building substance in our bodies, you can find them in every cell and tissue. Further, they are, among other things, responsible for muscle growth, the immune system and the regulation of hormones. You should have a daily intake of about 0.8–1g of protein per kg of bodyweight. When doing intense physical activities, you can aim for more – around 1.8–2g per kg of bodyweight. Building muscles just by eating more protein or losing fat this way is (unfortunately) a myth – this can only happen in combination with physical activity.

ESSENTIAL AMINO ACIDS

Proteins are composed of different amino acids that are, in chemical terms, long chains of small molecules. We need 20 different amino acids to metabolize protein. Nine of them are essential. Our body cannot produce those nine amino acids itself, so they have to be taken in with our food. Some proteins we eat contain all of these nine amino acids – we call them 'complete' or 'whole' proteins as they can theoretically cover the requirement of essential amino acids by themselves. In general, animal protein is considered whole and plant protein is considered incomplete. But there are exceptions: pseudo-grains like quinoa, amaranth and buckwheat as well as seeds like hemp, sunflower and pumpkin are plant-based sources of whole proteins. Nevertheless, this topic is important for vegans. If you have a balanced mixed diet, the amino acids usually complement each other automatically, for example when having hummus (legumes plus nuts/seeds). Vegans can take in all the essential amino acids by combining various different plant-based foods. When you match certain foods that have different incomplete amino acids, you can 'build' complete proteins, for example by combining rice with kidney beans or oats with peanuts. I like to include those combinations in my recipes as well, for example in the Vegan Protein Buddha Bowl (see page 139), which contains 25g of protein and all the essential amino acids.

THE CONNECTION BETWEEN PROTEIN AND HUNGER

Studies and experiments by scientists show that both animals and humans only eat until their protein requirement is covered. Carbohydrates and fats are not that important when it comes to being hungry. The problem with industrially made foods is that they are usually mixed with cheap sugars and fats. This automatically reduces their protein content, which means that the amount of protein is proportionally lower. That's why you're more likely to overeat and chronically stay hungry.

PROTEIN PRODUCTS I LIKE

Generally speaking, we can assume you will cover your daily protein requirement with a balanced, healthy diet. If you don't consume enough protein, or just want to use protein shakes as an addition, protein supplements may be your solution. The best known are protein powders that can be used in smoothies or for baking. Powders made from animal sources such as milk protein (casein protein) or whey protein are the most common kinds. However, there are great vegan alternatives. My favourites are pea, rice, peanut, flaxseed and hemp protein, but you can also get protein powder made from soy, seeds and other nuts.

There are also multi-component protein powders available that are a blend of different kinds and therefore offer the full amino acid spectrum. When buying protein powder, you should watch out for the ingredients and nutritional information. Usually the rule of thumb is: the fewer ingredients the better. Some manufacturers add sugar or sweeteners. That's not necessary at all, so I avoid these products. If I'd like to add sweetness to my shake, I can always use fresh fruit. I tend to get bloated from some protein powders. The same kind of another brand will work fine for me though. It's probably the level of processing, so be patient when finding a good one that works with your body!

Another product category is protein bars. It's also crucial to have a look at the ingredients list here! They might sound healthy, but often contain added sugar, sweeteners, artificial flavours and various chemical ingredients. You should consider them sweets in this case.

TIP:

Make sure you drink enough water when consuming protein shakes. People with medical conditions affecting the kidneys or their metabolism, as well as pregnant women, should only consume them to a limited extent, or not at all.

PLANT PROTEIN SOURCES – MY FAVOURITES (PROTEIN PER 100G):

Chickpeas (jar or can): c. 7g
Garden peas: c. 7g
Hemp seeds: c. 30g
Mushrooms: c. 3g
Oats: c. 12g
Peanuts: c. 27g
Quinoa (uncooked): c. 15g
Red lentils (uncooked): c. 25g
Spinach: c. 3g
Tahini: c. 17g

TIPS FOR A BETTER DIGESTION

Bloating

Fermentation of non-digestible food parts or swallowing air causes bloating. Even though the topic is not a 'pleasant' one to talk about, it's still a normal process and part of digestion. But it's only normal to a certain degree. If pain or other problems occur it can quickly turn into an uncomfortable matter. And you should not feel bloated every evening. During a small period of my life I thought it's 'normal' to be bloated at the end of the day – but it doesn't need to be. Luckily there are several ways to support and improve your digestion:

1. GIVE YOUR BODY TIME. If you are changing your diet and going for a more healthy, high-fibre and raw food diet your gut bacteria need to adjust slowly since they are not used to those kinds of foods. That's why bloating can occur, especially in the beginning of a change in diet. To prevent that from happening, the amount of fibre in your food should only be increased bit by bit.

2. THE RIGHT ORDER WHILE EATING. Personally, I feel good starting out with food that's easy to digest and contains a high water content like fruit, and finishing with foods that are harder to digest and contain only little water, for example high protein ones. Fruits as dessert sit heavily on my stomach and leave me with an unpleasant feeling. This applies especially to melons, which I therefore only eat on an empty stomach. I don't always stick to the right order because I enjoy combining different flavours. If you are struggling with digestion you should try to pay attention to it though.

3. DON'T DRINK WHILE EATING. I've noticed my digestion works way better and my food belly returns to being flat faster when I'm not drinking while eating. I also avoid drinking anything 20–30 minutes before and 1 hour after a big meal. If I am going out to eat I usually order a cup of warm tea in the beginning and politely reject any offer of another drink afterwards. A naturopathic doctor once told me that a cold drink 'is comparable to pouring cold water on a grill. You need to heat up the grill all over again before it will work properly'. I don't think it's a proven fact – but it definitely made sense to me.

4. CONSCIOUS CONSUMPTION. Eating deserves our full attention. If you get distracted by your phone or TV you might tend to eat too fast, which in return means you don't chew long enough, swallow more air or simply eat too much.

5. VEGETABLES AND FRUITS THAT CAUSE BLOATING include any kind of kale, legumes, garlic and onions which have, especially when raw, high amounts of non-digestible nutrients. To this day, I can still only consume limited portions of legumes and stay away from big servings of cauliflower and broccoli, if I don't want to risk bloating.

6. FOODS THAT ARE HARD TO DIGEST like, for example, very fatty, processed, high in sugar foods or processed animal products in general should be avoided.

7. FAT IS HARD TO DIGEST. Especially if you have a sensitive stomach you shouldn't mix different kinds of fats. Avocados, nuts and olives consumed together can be a problem for some of us. On the other hand, including a moderate amound of natural fat is very beneficial to get food through your body smoothly.

8. KEEPING A FOOD DIARY. If you feel like you're not doing well with a certain food or nutrient it can be very helpful to start a food diary, to keep track of what you are eating and how you respond to it. This way it's easier to tell which exact ingredient of your meal might cause you digestion problems, simply by the method of elimination. If you suspect you have intolerances or allergies, you should consult an expert.

9. DON'T OVEREAT! I'm speaking from a lot of experience here. When I am loading up on huge amounts of oats, quinoa, dates – which I tolerate well in normal quantities – it doesn't take long till my belly gets bloated. For a long time I tried to figure out what type of food causes me bloating – until I noticed it's not a specific food, it was the fact of overeating. Because everything was SO YUMMY to me! Sometimes the crucial aspect is not what you eat, but rather how much of it. So, if your head craves for more but your stomach is already full … you'd better learn how to stop.

SHOPPING TIPS

Think about the environment

Shop sustainably. The more I deal with the topic of nutrition, the clearer it gets to me that the 'right' way of eating is not only about me and my body, it's also about eating consciously and as sustainably as possible – for the sake of the environment and the planet. I strongly believe it's not about perfectionism here, but about the little things that will add up and make a big difference in the long run, especially when more and more people start to think about where and what they can do to make a small contribution to sustainability in everyday life. This might be reducing their meat consumption, buying local foods, no longer using disposable plastic bags when shopping, changing over to glass bottles or talking about the issue with friends and colleagues.

To me, these efforts also include paying attention to where my ingredients come from and how they are produced or farmed. I prefer buying my fruits and vegetables at the organic grocery store or the farmers' market. I am mindful of what's in season and locally grown. It's not about always being 100% consistent with this – I purchase frozen raspberries in winter and regularly eat bananas, too.

THINGS TO KNOW ABOUT ORGANIC PRODUCTS

Even though organic foods are not always healthier than regular foods, there are still a lot of positive facts: organic products are usually way less polluted by pesticides, farming is more sustainable and resource-conserving and animal farming is better for the animals in general. Still, not every organic certificate on a product means it's automatically 'better'.

The hexagonal European organic certificate ensures basic conditions, whilst other certificates require stricter standards to be met. Some, for example, prohibit monocultures, pesticides, nuclear radiation or genetically modified seeds. Each part of the world has different certificates ensuring that, so you should take a moment to research what applies in your country. I am aware these products are often more expensive than conventional foods. But if you have some financial wiggle room it should not hurt to go for ingredients with these organic certificates. You are what you eat. And the world is our only home. There's a solution for everyone who thinks that shopping at the organic grocery is too expensive in the long-term: a lot of supermarket chains offer their own lines of organic brands that are somewhat more affordable.

Check, of course, that the products at least meet the standard requirements, or really are of higher quality compared to the basic products as that's not always the case. It's worthwhile doing your research and, by purchasing organic products, setting an example for sustainable and ecological farming.

CAUTION WITH TRENDFOODS AND SUPERFOODS

When shopping it's also worth looking for simple alternatives to imported goods. Especially when talking about trendfoods or superfoods you should be aware of the possible consequences in their countries of origin. For example, excessive avocado farming is linked to water shortages in South America and, due to the quinoa boom, a lot of farmers in the countries that produce it and where it was a nourishing staple food, can no longer afford it.

Global products are not always bad, of course, but I prefer to buy them in moderation rather than in excess.

BASE INGREDIENTS

The following list gives you an idea about which ingredients you need for the recipes in this book. It also shows which ingredients I usually have available and the ones I buy regularly. For fruits and vegetables, my selection varies depending on the season.

FATS & OILS / NUTS, SEEDS & KERNELS

- Avocado oil
- Coconut oil
- Flax oil
- Nut butter (e.g. hazelnut, cashew or almond butter, peanut butter)
- Nuts (walnuts, almonds, peanuts, pine nuts, cashews, hazelnuts, pecans)
- Olive oil
- Seeds (pumpkin, flax, hemp and sunflower seeds)
- Tahini (sesame paste)

FRUITS

- Fruits
- Apples
- Bananas
- Berries (seasonal: strawberries, raspberries and so on – also frozen)
- Dates
- Dried fruits (e.g. raisins, dried apples rings)
- Figs
- Grapes with seeds
- Lemons
- Mangos (fresh or frozen)
- Pears
- Plums

GRAINS, PSEUDO-GRAINS & LEGUMES

- Beans (e.g. black beans, mung beans)
- Buckwheat
- Chickpeas (canned)
- Coconut or almond flour
- Lentils
- Oats
- Pasta (made from wholegrain flour or legumes)
- (Puffed) Quinoa
- Rice (e.g. basmati or brown rice)
- Whole spelt flour

SUPERFOODS

- Açaí purée (frozen)
- Chia seeds
- Cocoa nibs
- Cocoa powder (low fat, raw)
- Coconut chips and grated coconut
- Coconut water
- Goji berries, mulberries
- Psyllium husks
- Spirulina powder
- Wheatgrass powder

VEGETABLES

- Artichoke hearts
- Avocado
- Beansprouts
- Beetroot
- Broccoli
- Carrots
- Corn (canned)
- Cucumber
- Ginger
- Lettuce (rocket, edible wild herbs, lamb's lettuce etc.)
- Mushrooms
- Olives
- Peas
- Peppers
- Potatoes and sweet potatoes
- Pumpkin
- Radishes
- Red cabbage
- (Baby) Spinach (fresh or frozen)
- Spring onions
- Tomatoes (fresh, dried, passata)
- Zucchini

MILK ALTERNATIVES & PROTEIN PRODUCTS

- Almond, cashew, oat or rice milk
- Cashew, almond or coconut yoghurt
- Coconut drink (around 8% coconut)
- Creamy coconut milk with high fat content (around 60% coconut)
- Protein powder (e.g. hemp, flaxseed or pea protein)

SPICES

- Bourbon vanilla, powder (not vanilla sugar)
- Cardamom, ground
- Ceylon cinnamon, ground
- Chilli powder
- Cumin, ground
- Ginger (fresh or ground)
- Nutmeg, grated
- Paprika, sweet
- Pepper
- Sea salt or Himalayan salt
- Turmeric, ground

HERBS (FRESH, FROZEN, DRIED)

- Basil
- Chives
- Dill
- Oregano
- Parsley
- Rosemary
- Thyme

SWEET THINGS

- Apple purée
- Bars (protein and nut bars etc.)
- Coconut blossom sugar
- Dark chocolate (85–92% cocoa)
- Honey
- Syrups (e.g. agave, date, maple)

ANIMAL PRODUCTS

- Beef fillet
- Chicken breast
- Eggs
- Minced meat (beef)

BOWL KNOWLEDGE

Basic bowl hacks

THIS IS HOW SMOOTHIE BOWLS TURN OUT CREAMY

◆ **AVOCADO:** Has a lot to offer, even in smaller quantities as it contains healthy fats, lots of vitamins and even more potassium than the well-loved banana! A great low-carb and low-sugar alternative.

◆ **BANANA – THE CLASSIC:** Provides natural sweetness and quickly accessible energy. You don't have ripe, sweet bananas at home? Just place whole yellow bananas – with the skin – in your oven and let them 'ripen' for 15–20 minutes on a high heat (160°C).

◆ **FROZEN ZUCCHINI:** The 'invisible' banana. You don't taste it, the result is almost as creamy and you can save some calories, carbohydrates and sugar. You are also smuggling in a portion of vegetables. That's why you can almost always find some stewed zucchini in my freezer. To prepare these, cut a zucchini into slices about 2cm thick, stew them in a pan for 5–10 minutes, then place the slices on some paper towels and let them cool. To prevent the slices sticking to one another, freeze them on a plate in a single layer and, once they're frozen, transfer them to a bag.

◆ **ICE CUBES:** Result in a nice ice cream texture. Of course, they don't add any calories.

◆ **NUT BUTTER:** One scoop does not only provide creaminess but also a nutty flavour.

EVEN MORE INGREDIENTS FOR BOWLS

◆ **APPLE CIDER VINEGAR:** This may sound weird at first, but a little shot of apple cider vinegar is part of my morning routine. It supports both digestion and the immune system and helps keep the blood sugar level and pH value in balance. That's why you can find this ingredient in some dressings.

◆ **COCOA:** Do you love chocolate flavour? Two teaspoons of cocoa powder per bowl is enough! Besides, cocoa provides antioxidants, stabilizes blood sugar and increases our feeling of happiness. It should be raw, de-oiled and without any additives though – also no added sugar.

◆ **COCONUT WATER:** This is nature's sports drink. It has isotonic properties and contains electrolytes. Heavy sweating can cause a loss of liquid and electrolytes and that's exactly what coconut water compensates for in a natural way.

◆ **FLAXSEEDS:** Fibre is our best friend! That's why flaxseeds play such an important role in this bowl cookbook. They are great for the digestion and keep us full for longer – that's how they prevent hunger attacks. Two teaspoons also provide us with our daily requirement of omega-3 fatty acids!

- **HEMP PROTEIN POWDER:** A great vegan source of protein! To produce it, hemp seeds are ground and partially de-oiled. The final hemp protein is usually not super highly processed. It also 'only' features a protein content of 45%, but to make up for that, it offers all essential amino acids, lots of fibre and an optimal ratio of omega-3 to omega-6 fatty acids.

WELL PREPARED

To be able to cook a delicious bowl at any time it's helpful to have some basic ingredients always available. Also, you need frozen fruits and vegetables for some of the recipes from the smoothie bowl chapter. I go for bananas quite often – cut them into pieces, freeze and briefly defrost before using. Berries, mango and peas can be bought frozen. Buy zucchini and sweet potato fresh, stew and freeze yourself.

WHILE COOKING

To prevent anything from getting stuck in the blender, add the liquids first, then the solid ingredients.

PREPARATION OF RECIPES IN TWO WAYS (GENERIC EXAMPLE)

Recipes like porridge can either be cooked as a version to lose weight, or as a version to gain weight. This may sound strange but works! With some slight changes to the ingredients:

HIGH-CALORIE PORRIDGE BOWL	LOW-CALORIE PORRIDGE BOWL
Cook with: Plant milk	Cook with: Water
Mix in: 1–2 tbsp nut butter	Mix in: 1 handful grated zucchini, 2–3 tbsp psyllium husks or crushed flaxseeds – they increase the volume and keep you full
Fruits: Bananas, dates or dried fruit	Fruits: Berries and other fresh fruits
Toppings: generous amount of seeds or nuts, nut butter	Toppings: Fresh fruits, puffed grains or berry jam (see page 213)

HOW TO START

Clean your kitchen

In my recipes I generally use ingredients that work the best for me and are, in my opinion, healthier than the common, standard option. Here's a list of which healthy ingredients I use to substitute them. Of course, everything is allowed now and then! But for daily consumption, the ingredients on the left side of the table are less suitable. So I would recommend putting these common ingredients, if you own them, all the way at the back of the cupboard. Because if you can't see them, it's easier not to use them too often!

THIS INGREDIENT ...	... REPLACED WITH:
HEAVILY PROCESSED PEANUT BUTTER	Natural peanut butter: Yes, not all peanut butters are created equal. Lots of them have sugar, palm or sunflower oil added to them. So always check the ingredients! There's no need for anything other than peanuts and salt. The same goes for any other kind of nut butter.
READY MEALS	Vegetables or legumes, canned or frozen: Always available and ready to use, whenever you want to cook something that's quick and delicious.
COW'S MILK YOGHURT	Plant-based yoghurt: I avoid dairy products for health and ethical reasons (find more on this topic on page 34, Milk & Alternatives).
COW'S MILK	Plant or nut milk: Because of the reasons stated above I prefer plant or nut milk.

THIS INGREDIENT ...	... REPLACED WITH:
JASMINE RICE	Brown rice: Is a wholegrain product and full of complex carbohydrates that get digested quite slowly. Jasmine rice causes the blood sugar to spike drastically. Alternatives: Millet or pseudo-grains like quinoa.
ICE CREAM	Nice cream: Made from bananas and other frozen fruits. It contains only natural ingredients and little fat (see recipe on page 177).
WHITE TABLE SUGAR	Coconut blossom sugar: Contains lots of minerals, is absorbed slower and is therefore healthier. Alternatives: maple syrup, date syrup, agave syrup, honey (find out more on page 42, Sugar & Alternatives).
WHITE FLOUR	Wholegrain flour, almond, oat or coconut flour: they contain more minerals and keep you full and satisfied for longer.
WHITE PASTA	Wholegrain pasta: All the good substances are located in or directly underneath the husk of the grain. When processing a grain until it's white flour, almost all the nutrients are lost. Alternative: zoodles.

KITCHEN UTENSILS, MACHINES AND TOOLS

To cook the recipes in this book, you will need the following:

Baking tray and baking parchment, bowls, chopping board, dehydrator (optional), food processor, freezer-proof containers, frying pan, hand mixer, high-power blender, knife, measuring cup with accurate scale, ovenproof dishes, vegetable peeler, pots and saucepans, pressure cooker (optional), grater, salad spinner, accurate kitchen scales (digital), (fine) sieve, spatula, spiral vegetable slicer, various containers (jars, glasses and boxes), whisk, cooking spoon.

Breakfast Bowls

2

Breakfast is by far my favourite meal of the day! Its name comes from 'breaking the fast', the night-time period when you do not consume any food – so it describes the first meal of the day. This also means you don't have to eat it in the morning, right? Personally, I don't feel hungry in the morning, but I would never want to skip my beloved porridge. So I simply enjoy it at midday or in the evening. Especially pre- or post-workout, porridge provides me with the energy I need. That's also why I love 'breakfast-all-day' restaurants when travelling! In the recipes on the following pages my love of porridge will become more than obvious. Some of you might be surprised at how versatile oats can actually be! Besides the sweet Breakfast Bowls – in which I only use fruits as natural sweeteners – you will also find some savoury bowls.

4-Ingredient Porridge – THE CLASSIC

about 10 mins

- *1/2 banana*
- *50g oats*
- *150ml plant milk*
- *1 tbsp nut butter (favourite: peanut butter)*
- *optional: ground Ceylon cinnamon or vanilla powder*

TOPPINGS:

- *1/2 banana, 1 tbsp nut butter*

Tip

* *Oats* are gluten-free, but they can come into contact with other grains during the packaging process. If you have a severe intolerance you should choose gluten-free oats.

1 Mash half of the banana with a fork – I like to use ripe bananas that are already a little brown.

2 Next, mix the mashed banana with the oats, plant milk and nut butter. This would also be the right moment to add some cinnamon or vanilla.

3 Simmer this mixture in a small saucepan on the stove for around 3 minutes to create a porridge.

4 For the toppings, slice the second half of the banana and add some more nut butter.

Oats every day & in every way – the headline to my life. I tried my best to create a lot of variety in this chapter, but porridge remains my favourite. This 4-Ingredient Porridge definitely shows how simple a delicious and creamy porridge can be. Let me warn you – there is a high risk of addiction! I can also warmly (or coldly) recommend the 'overnight porridge' version. To do so, skip step 3 and let the mixture soak overnight in the fridge. To find out what these healthy, inexpensive oats can do, go to page 28.

NUTRITIONAL VALUES APPROX. 440 KCAL – 13G PROTEIN – 54G CARBOHYDRATES – 10G FIBRE – 18G FAT (15G UNSATURATED)

PEANUT BUTTER & JELLY
Porridge Bowl

about 25 mins

- *1/2 apple or 1/2 banana*
- *50g oats*
- *150ml water*
- *100ml plant milk (e.g. oat milk)*
- *1 pinch of salt*
- *2 tsp peanut butter*
- *optional: 1 tbsp agave, maple or date syrup*

TOPPINGS:

- *50g berry jam (recipe on page 213), 1 tsp peanut butter, some berries and 10g peanuts.*

Tip

* Is your *peanut butter* too hard or sticky? Simply add a dash of hot water and mix well.

1 For the topping, you'll need berry jam. You can prepare it fresh or use some you made earlier and have stored in the fridge. The homemade jam will last for 3 to 4 days after opening (recipe on page 213).

2 Finely chop or shred the apple. Alternatively, you could mash half a banana and add it here instead.

3 Add the fruit, oats, water, 50ml plant milk and salt to a saucepan and warm over low heat while stirring constantly. Take it off the heat after 3 minutes and stir in some peanut butter and the remaining plant milk. If you like it a little sweeter, you can always add one teaspoon of the sweeteners listed!

4 Pour the porridge into a bowl and top it with the berry jam and more peanut butter. I also like to add some fresh berries and peanuts.

The PB&J Bowl is already well-known thanks to my food channel on Instagram. The inspiration for this recipe is of course found in the US where peanut butter and jelly is a true classic on toast and in sandwiches. The flavours of this sweet 'n' salty combination are the same here, but with natural ingredients and without any additional sugars. And this also applies to the homemade berry jam!

NUTRITIONAL VALUES APPROX. 490 KCAL – 16G PROTEIN – 53G CARBOHYDRATES – 11G FIBRE – 22G FAT (19G UNSATURATED)

WARM NUT PORRIDGE
with Fried Fruits

about 10 mins

- *20g nuts and seeds (e.g. almonds and pumpkin seeds)*
- *3–4 thin slices of ginger*
- *50g oats*
- *2 tsp smaller seeds (e.g. flaxseeds and hemp seeds)*
- *1 pinch of salt*
- *100ml water*
- *1 tsp ground Ceylon cinnamon*
- *vanilla powder*
- *100ml plant milk (oat or rice milk)*

TOPPINGS:

- *100g fruit (e.g. bananas, apples or plums), 1 tsp coconut oil, ground Ceylon cinnamon, vanilla powder*

Info

* To find out why nuts and seeds are so healthy, look on page 38.

1 Roughly chop the nuts and seeds and mince the ginger slices as finely as possible. Alternatively, use ground ginger.

2 Place the nuts, seeds, oats, salt, water, spices and 50ml of the plant milk in a saucepan and simmer over low heat for 3 minutes. Take the saucepan off the heat and mix in the remaining plant milk.

3 Wash, clean and/or peel the fruit as necessary and cut in small pieces. In a frying pan, sauté the fruit in the coconut oil, cinnamon and vanilla. If using hard fruit (e.g. apples), add some water. This helps the spices to disperse and the fruit will become nice and soft.

4 Pour the porridge into a bowl and dress with the fried fruits.

Frying fruit with cinnamon and vanilla wasn't my idea. My mum has been doing it for years, especially with apples and bananas. And each time she does, our home smells of baked apples and bananas. Compared with a classic baked apple this recipe won't give you a bad conscience – it tastes good even without adding sugar or butter. You know what my mum loves as well? Nuts. That's why we can call this dish 'Mum's favourite' – just like the Coconut-Banana-Cake recipe on page 191.

NUTRITIONAL VALUES APPROX. 498 KCAL – 16G PROTEIN – 54G CARBOHYDRATES – 11G FIBRE – 24G FAT (17G UNSATURATED)

FIG CINNAMON PORRIDGE
with Homemade Fig Jam

about 25 mins

- *50g fig and pecan jam (recipe on page 214)*
- *1/2 apple*
- *3–4 very fine slices of ginger*
- *50g oats*
- *150ml water*
- *150ml plant milk (e.g. oat milk)*
- *1 tsp crushed flaxseeds*
- *1 tsp ground Ceylon cinnamon*

TOPPINGS:

- *1 small fig, 10g pecan nuts, 1 tsp cocoa nibs*

1 Make the fig and pecan jam from scratch. You can prepare it fresh for this recipe or you may already have some stored in your fridge. The recipe is on page 214.

2 Wash the apple and ginger and cut them into small pieces. Alternatively, you can use 1/2 tsp ground ginger.

3 Put the apple and ginger pieces with the oats, water, 100ml plant milk, flaxseeds and cinnamon into a saucepan. Warm over low heat while stirring constantly. After 3 minutes, take it off the heat and stir in the remaining plant milk and the jam, but remember to leave some jam for the topping!

4 Wash the fig, cut it into pieces and use to decorate your porridge with some pecan nuts, cocoa nibs and the remaining jam.

Jam can do so much more than just be a spread for bread! It also tastes like a dream in combination with oats and is a welcome change to my beloved nut butter. By the way, figs belong to the oldest fruits consumed by mankind. Cleopatra's favourite fruit is rich in essential minerals like magnesium, copper and calcium. Dried figs contain even more calcium than milk! Also, the riper the fig, the more antioxidants it contains.

Tip

* If the *figs* are fresh, you can even eat their skin!

NUTRITIONAL VALUES APPROX. 617 KCAL – 12G PROTEIN – 75G CARBOHYDRATES – 17G FIBRE – 29G FAT (23G UNSATURATED)

Yum

BANANA BREAD PORRIDGE *with Rawnola*

about 10 mins

- *1 ripe banana*
- *40g oats*
- *1 tsp crushed flaxseeds*
- *1 tbsp chopped hazelnuts*
- *1 tbsp raisins*
- *150ml plant milk*
- *100ml water*
- *1 pinch of salt*
- *1 tsp ground Ceylon cinnamon*
- *vanilla powder*
- *1/4 tsp ground cardamom*

TOPPINGS:

- *20g Ultimate Rawnola (find the recipe on page 204), 1 tsp honey*

Note

* The browner the *banana*, the better! Ripe bananas are sweeter and perfectly suited to this recipe.

1 Cut a quarter of the banana into slices and set aside for the topping. Mash the remaining banana with a fork.

2 In a saucepan, slowly heat the mashed banana with the oats, flaxseeds, hazelnuts, raisins, plant milk, water, salt and spices.

3 Let it simmer for about 3 minutes and stir regularly.

4 Pour the porridge into a bowl and dress with the banana slices, rawnola (I used the Ultimate Rawnola from page 204) and some honey.

I love baking banana bread – but who has the time to bake on a daily basis? With this porridge you can create the flavours of banana bread in just 10 minutes! I enjoy this porridge when I am relaxing at home with cosy socks, a hot-water bottle and a scented candle. Of course, you can make this recipe vegan by replacing the honey with date syrup or coconut blossom sugar.

If you enjoy your porridge less sticky, you can always add more plant milk or water. This really depends on your own preference. As always in life: some like it thick, some like it ... creamy.

NUTRITIONAL VALUES APPROX. 502 KCAL – 12G PROTEIN – 67G CARBOHYDRATES – 11G FIBRE – 19G FAT (15G UNSATURATED)

VANILLA QUINOA PORRIDGE – *Autumn in a Bowl*

about 35 mins

- *100g squash*
- *1 tsp coconut oil*
- *2 tsp ground Ceylon cinnamon*
- *80g uncooked quinoa (equals about 250g cooked)*
- *150ml plant milk (oat or rice milk)*
- *100ml water*
- *1 pinch of salt*
- *vanilla powder*
- *1/4 tsp ground cardamom*
- *1–2 tsp date or maple syrup*

TOPPINGS:

- *2 small figs, 1 handful of grapes*

Info

* *Quinoa* exists in lots of varieties – the three most common ones are white, red and black. Out of these, white quinoa tastes the mildest.

1 Preheat the oven to 180°C.

2 Cut the squash into pieces and remove the seeds. Coat the pieces with coconut oil and sprinkle them with 1 tsp of the cinnamon. Bake for 20–30 minutes on a baking tray lined with baking parchment. Depending on the size of your pieces, the duration may vary.

3 Meanwhile, wash the quinoa and add it to a saucepan. Bring it to a boil with the plant milk, water, salt, vanilla, cardamom and the remaining cinnamon over medium heat. Afterwards, reduce the heat and let it simmer for 15 minutes. Take the saucepan off the stove, cover with a lid and let it sit until the squash is done. Season the porridge with date or maple syrup to taste before serving.

4 Pour the quinoa porridge into a bowl. Dress with the cleaned and cut up figs, grapes and the roasted cinnamon-squash.

The colder and more unpleasant the weather becomes during autumn, the nicer the smell of roasted cinnamon-squash, which is slowly spreading at home. Squash and quinoa are both better known for savoury recipes, but taste amazing in combination with sweet flavours as well! Quinoa also works great as a substitute for oats to make a porridge – give it a try!

NUTRITIONAL VALUES APPROX. 562 KCAL – 16G PROTEIN – 94G CARBOHYDRATES – 12G FIBRE – 11G FAT (6G UNSATURATED)

RAWNOLA BOWL

about 10 mins

- *50g rawnola (e.g. Fruit Rawnola see page 207)*
- *150ml plant milk*

1 Make the rawnola yourself. You can find the detailed instructions and two variations on pages 204 and 207. It tastes even better if you prepare it one day ahead but, in an 'emergency', it can easily be done in 10 minutes – so don't worry.

2 Grab your favourite plant milk and enjoy immediately! If you wait for too long, the rawnola could get soggy.

I ate muesli with milk for breakfast throughout my entire childhood. And yes, I was already looking forward to it the evening before, while lying in bed. These days, classic muesli mixtures or ready-made granolas contain vast amounts of sugar so that they taste better. This even applies to products available from organic stores. In the long run, this actually results in bigger cravings for sweet stuff: our taste buds adjust to the level of sweetness super-quickly, making everything else taste bland and boring. I never shop for muesli without checking the list of ingredients. Cane sugar, rice syrup, maltose, dextrose, glucose and fructose syrup – these are just some terms to look out for. Also palm fat, inexpensive sunflower oil, flavourings and emulsifiers are commonly found in crunchy muesli. In low quantities that's acceptable for sure, but a whole bowl every morning is too much. Check page 42 if you want to read more about sugar.

NUTRITIONAL VALUES APPROX. 217 KCAL – 6G PROTEIN – 28G CARBOHYDRATES – 8G FIBRE – 8G FAT (6G UNSATURATED)

Note

* My Fruit Rawnola is easy to make at home and turns out great without any syrup, added sugar or oil. Instead, it contains dried fruit, important vitamins and a lot of fibre. A healthy breakfast and truly a treat in the morning!

Creamy Buckwheat RICE PUDDING

about 25 mins
+ optional: soaking for 1 hour minimum

- *50g uncooked buckwheat (equals about 90g of soaked buckwheat)*
- *100ml creamy coconut milk (about 60% coconut)*
- *100ml water*
- *1 pinch of salt*
- *grated nutmeg*
- *1 tsp ground Ceylon cinnamon*
- *vanilla powder*
- *50g fruit (e.g. apple, pear, banana)*
- *10g raisins*
- *20g nuts (e.g. almonds and hazelnuts)*
- *optional: 1 tsp date, maple or agave syrup*

Food Swaps

* If you want to reduce calories or don't have creamy coconut milk at hand, you can also use plant milk and some apple purée instead!

1 Let the buckwheat simmer in a saucepan with the coconut milk, water, salt and spices for about 20 minutes. If you soak the buckwheat for about 1 hour in a bowl of water beforehand, cooking will only take around 10–15 minutes.

2 In the meantime, clean the fruit, peel if necessary and cut it into little pieces. Chop the nuts. Put some of the fruit, nuts and raisins aside to use later as a topping. Throw what's left into the saucepan with the buckwheat and let that simmer for 5 minutes over a low heat.

3 Season the rice pudding once again with the spices. If you would prefer more sweetness, mix in some date, maple or agave syrup.

4 Pour everything into a bowl and top the pudding with the fruit, nuts and raisins that you put aside earlier.

Buckwheat has been cultivated for over 5,000 years and is a daily part of the Russian diet, but has long been forgotten in other parts of the world. It has a nutty flavour, is gluten-free and is not related to common wheat. It is rich in slowly digested carbohydrates, vitamins and minerals. That's why 100g buckwheat provides over 50% of your daily requirements of manganese and about 25% of your daily requirement of magnesium, which among other things benefits your blood sugar and blood pressure.

NUTRITIONAL VALUES APPROX. 558 KCAL – 11G PROTEIN – 59G CARBOHYDRATES – 7G FIBRE – 31G FAT (11G UNSATURATED)

CHOCOLATE-RASPBERRY PUDDING
with Chia Seeds

about 20 mins

- *15g chia seeds*
- *1 tsp raw, low-fat cocoa powder*
- *1 pinch of salt*
- *1/2 tsp ground Ceylon cinnamon*
- *1/2 ripe banana*
- *25g avocado*
- *50ml creamy coconut milk (around 60% coconut)*
- *50ml plant milk (coconut or almond milk)*
- *50g raspberries*
- *optional: 1 tsp date or maple syrup, honey*

1 In a bowl, mix the chia seeds, cocoa powder, salt and cinnamon.

2 Blend the banana and avocado until creamy and add to the chia seeds.

3 Then pour the coconut and plant milk onto the mixture and give it a good stir. If desired, add some date syrup, maple syrup or honey.

4 As a last step mix in the fresh or frozen raspberries while keeping some aside for the topping. In the beginning the consistency will seem too runny but after about 15 minutes the chia seeds will have soaked and create the wonderful, creamy texture to the pudding.

For a chia pudding we use the immense swelling properties of chia seeds. Usually I am an advocate for local flaxseeds but I admit, chia seeds are best suited to this recipe. Their taste is neutral, and that's why they are a great base to create delicious flavours with some extra ingredients. The avocado and banana are responsible for the creaminess. This recipe might be low in calories and carbs, but it will still keep you full for a long time. It is also very rich in important nutrients like vitamins and minerals.

Food Swaps: You can replace the avocado by the same amount of banana!

NUTRITIONAL VALUES APPROX. 310 KCAL – 7G PROTEIN – 18G CARBOHYDRATES – 6G FIBRE – 21G FAT (10G UNSATURATED)

Note

* This recipe works also as an Overnight Pudding. Just prepare it in the evening and let it soak overnight in the fridge, ready to be enjoyed the next day.

e up - Breakfast time

SWEET SCRAMBLED EGGS
with Banana & Coconut

about 15 mins

- *1 banana*
- *2 medium eggs*
- *2 tbsp creamy coconut milk (around 60% coconut)*
- *1 tsp coconut oil*

TOPPINGS:

- *1 tsp flaked coconut, 10g chopped almonds, 2 tsp nut butter (e.g. almond), 1/2 pear*

Info

* *Eggs* from chickens that live outdoors contain more vitamins and healthy omega-3 fatty acids!

1 Peel the banana and cut into pieces. Ideally, use a very ripe banana with some brown spots.

2 In a bowl, whisk the eggs and add the coconut milk. I prefer using creamy coconut milk which contains around 60% coconut.

3 Put aside some banana slices for the topping. Add the remaining pieces to the eggs and stir. Sauté in a frying pan with some coconut oil. I like my scrambled eggs the best when they're not well done, but still a little soft.

4 Dress the scrambled eggs with the flaked coconut, almonds and add some nut butter. Slice the pear and put it on top of the eggs with the remaining banana.

Sweet scrambled eggs? This may sound like an unusual pairing, but banana and eggs actually go together really well. The banana becomes really soft when fried and its sugar caramelizes in the pan – which makes it taste even stronger and sweeter! This is another dish that I learned from my mum – she cooks it several times a week. That's why I have always regarded this combination of flavours as 'normal', even if it may raise a few eyebrows out there.

Food Swaps: If you don't have creamy coconut milk, you can replace it with the same amount of coconut yoghurt.

NUTRITIONAL VALUES APPROX. 524 KCAL – 20G PROTEIN – 35G CARBOHYDRATES – 7G FIBRE – 34G FAT (18G UNSATURATED)

SPINACH-CHICKPEA PATTIES
with a Poached Egg

about 15 mins

- *100g cherry tomatoes*
- *50g avocado*
- *60g canned chickpeas*
- *3 medium eggs*
- *1 splash of lemon juice*
- *grated nutmeg*
- *1 big pinch of salt*
- *pepper*
- *20g fresh baby spinach*
- *1 tsp avocado oil*
- *1 tsp vinegar*
- *2 tsp tahini (sesame paste)*

NUTRITIONAL VALUES APPROX.
548 KCAL –
30G PROTEIN –
16G CARBOHYDRATES –
10G FIBRE – 39G FAT
(26G UNSATURATED)

1 Wash the tomatoes and dice them. Cut the avocado into small pieces and set aside.

2 Rinse the chickpeas thoroughly in a strainer. Using a blender or food processor, mix them with two of the eggs, the lemon juice, nutmeg, salt and pepper to create a batter.

3 Clean and wash the spinach, shake dry and tear the leaves into pieces. Add them to the batter and fold in.

4 Pour some avocado oil into a frying pan and start to sauté small, round patties. Turn them and wait till both sides are golden brown.

5 Into a bowl, break the third egg, making sure not to burst the yolk. Add water to a saucepan until it is half full. Add the vinegar and bring to a simmer. Lower the heat and stir with a spoon, creating a kind of whirlpool. Carefully place the egg in the middle of the whirlpool and let it sit for 3–4 minutes. Thanks to the movement of the water, the egg white folds and hardens around the egg yolk.

6 Serve the tomatoes, avocados, patties and the poached egg in a bowl, seasoned with salt and pepper.

7 As a sauce, simply use pure tahini (sesame butter) or thin it with a little water.

SCRAMBLED EGGS
with Veggies & Roasted Buckwheat

about 15 mins

- *100g zucchini*
- *50g mushrooms*
- *1 tsp avocado oil*
- *ground chilli*
- *salt and pepper*
- *100g cherry tomatoes*
- *1 handful of fresh parsley*
- *3 medium eggs*
- *20g buckwheat*

Tip

* This base recipe for scrambled eggs is suited for using all the leftover veggies you can find in your fridge. Feel inspired and get creative!

1 Clean the zucchini and mushrooms and cut them into small pieces. Place them in a frying pan and sauté with some avocado oil; season to taste with chilli powder, salt and pepper. Then wash and dice the tomatoes. Wash the parsley, shake dry and chop roughly. Add both to the veggies.

2 In the meantime, whisk the eggs in a bowl. Add them to the veggies and fry all together. The veggies should already look a bit roasted and brown.

3 Roast the dry buckwheat without any fat in a separate, non-stick pan over low heat for about 2–3 minutes. Toss regularly and serve when golden brown.

4 Season the eggs to your liking, put them in a bowl and sprinkle the roasted buckwheat on top.

On the fitness scene, a low-calorie and low-fat version using just the egg white would probably be more popular – but I don't like leaving out the golden egg yolk, since this would also mean leaving out 90% of all the nutrients and vitamins. Also, the egg yolk contains the so called 'sun's vitamin' – vitamin D – which is rarely found in food and which a lot of people lack. But what's even more important to me: organic free-range farming!

NUTRITIONAL VALUES APPROX. 389 KCAL – 25G PROTEIN – 23G CARBOHYDRATES – 5G FIBRE – 21G FAT (12G UNSATURATED)

Oven-Baked LOW-CARB EGG

about 30 mins

- *50g vegetables (e.g. sweet pepper and spinach)*
- *2 medium eggs*
- *salt*
- *pepper*
- *ground chilli*
- *1 tsp avocado oil*

TOPPINGS:

- *1 tsp olive oil*

Tip

* Too few calories? No problem. Just add some feta to the veggies or choose a creamy avocado as a side – both fit beautifully with the base recipe. Low-carb can be really delicious!

1 Preheat oven to 180°C.

2 A big variety of vegetables work well in this recipe – tomatoes, zucchini, olives or mushrooms. Just have a look at what's in your fridge! I used red pepper and spinach. Clean both, dice the pepper and chop the spinach roughly.

3 Whisk 1 of the eggs with a fork, add the veggies, mix everything and season with salt, pepper and chilli powder. Now take a small ovenproof dish, grease it with the avocado oil and pour in the veggie and egg mix.

4 Spread the mixture to create a hole in the middle of the bowl. Break the second egg right into this hole.

5 Bake for 20–25 minutes in the oven, then top with a little olive oil and enjoy!

Frying, poaching, cooking eggs – everyone knows those methods. But have you baked eggs in the oven before? It takes a little longer than usual but you can use this time productively … for example by doing your hair and make-up! That makes it a perfect dish for the daily, stressful morning routine, since the actual time spent for preparing is 5 minutes max. It's also ideal for everyone enjoying a low-carb diet!

NUTRITIONAL VALUES APPROX. 259 KCAL – 16G PROTEIN – 3G CARBOHYDRATES – 1G FIBRE – 20G FAT (13G UNSATURATED)

Smoothie Bowls

3

Smoothie Bowls are a food trend that has a high potential to stick around long-term if you ask me. I run into them wherever I travel – whether it's Bali, London or L.A. A smoothie bowl is based on a very thick smoothie that's served with all kinds of toppings and enjoyed immediately. The result is a rather sweet dish that's creamy, refreshingly light and usually fruity in flavour. Smoothie Bowls are healthy, they look super beautiful and don't take long to prepare – you just need a blender. They also provide you with energy quickly because blended, creamy ingredients can be processed by our bodies very easily.

AÇAÍ BOWL

about 10 mins

- *100g frozen açaí purée*
- *1 banana*
- *50ml plant milk*

TOPPINGS:

- *1/2 banana, 1 handful berries, some almonds, 2 tsp flaked coconut*

NUTRITIONAL VALUES APPROX.

390 KCAL –
7G PROTEIN –
46G CARBOHYDRATES –
12G FIBRE –
21G FAT (12G UNSATURATED)

Info

* Unbelievable but true: the *açaí* berry contains 0g of sugar!

1 In a blender, mix the açaí purée with the banana – fresh or frozen – and the plant milk.

2 For the toppings – get creative! Usually I slice 1/2 a banana, garnish with a handful of berries, some almonds and flaked coconut in a way that creates the typical açaí-bowl stripes.

I sell my own açaí purée in German supermarkets for a reason. That is also why I am kind of biased concerning this topic. Regardless, I like to talk and inform people about the health benefits and special traits of açaí. First off: choose frozen açaí purée over powder. When frozen, açaí is fresher and still contains almost all its vitamins and nutrients. Also – it tastes way better! The açaí berries for my purée are picked in Brazil from açaí palm trees. This means the palm trees are not being cut down and the rainforest needs to stay intact, healthy and protected. Since the seeds make up to around 90% of the berry, they are seeded and then processed to a mash. If it's high-quality açaí, the purée is flash-frozen right away to preserve the nutrients. Açaí is extremely rich in antioxidant properties which can be expressed on the ORAC scale (see page 9). Açaí reaches a value of over 100,000, while blueberries only reach around 9,000 and an apple just about 3,000. Please find out more about antioxidants on page 49. To bring this information overload to an end: açai bowls taste incredibly delicious and, from my experience, even men like them.

CHOCOLATE-AÇAÍ BOWL – *No-Banana Version*

about 10 mins

- *50g frozen, mixed berries*
- *50g frozen mango*
- *100g frozen açaí purée*
- *2 tsp raw, low-fat cocoa powder*
- *100ml plant milk*

TOPPINGS:

- *20g frozen mango, some raspberries, 2 tsp cocoa nibs, some mulberries, 1 tsp bee pollen.*

Info

* *Mangos* belong to the group of fruits with the highest concentration of vitamin A and contain comparable amounts of vitamin C to lemons!

1 In a blender, mix the berries, mango, açaí purée, cocoa powder and plant milk of your choice until smooth and creamy.

2 Pour into a bowl and dress however you like. I like to garnish my chocolate-açaí bowl with pieces of frozen mango, raspberries, cocoa nibs, mulberries and bee pollen – arranged in stripes.

Yes, an açaí bowl can be made without bananas. That's the answer to one of the most common questions I am asked about my beloved açaí purée. Frozen mango and frozen berries are a great alternative and add an even more exotic taste to the bowl. And what a surprise: I love to add some cocoa, transforming this creation into a chocolate bowl. I don't dare to claim this to be a 'trick' – using cocoa powder seems way too simple. The healthy properties of cocoa powder further enhance the anti-ageing effect of the açaí berry with its huge antioxidant content. For glowing skin and a strong immune system! Find more about antioxidants on page 49.

NUTRITIONAL VALUES APPROX. 292 KCAL – 8G PROTEIN – 21G CARBOHYDRATES – 9G FIBRE – 17G FAT (10G UNSATURATED)

CREAMY SWEET POTATO
Smoothie Bowl

about 70 mins

- *200g sweet potato*
- *300ml plant milk (oat or rice milk work the best)*
- *50ml creamy coconut milk (about 60% coconut)*
- *1 pinch of salt*
- *1 tsp ground Ceylon cinnamon*
- *ground cardamom*
- *grated nutmeg*
- *optional: 2 tbsp plant protein powder (my recommendation: flaxseed protein), 1 stoned date if you like*

TOPPINGS:

- *1 handful of blueberries*

Tip

* In the warmer months I prepare the sweet potato and freeze it in slices so I can mix a refreshing variation of this recipe. The consistency reminds me of ice cream!

1 Preheat the oven to 180°C. Clean the sweet potato. Prick some holes in the skin using a fork, then put the whole potato on a baking tray lined with baking parchment and bake for 30–60 minutes – depending on the size. Let it cool for a couple of minutes. If you want to, you can now peel the potato, though I like to leave the skin on. My favourite alternative method to baking in the oven is cooking in a pressure cooker. To do so, I clean the potato and cook it whole for 15 minutes. Even boiling is possible – all that matters is that the sweet potato becomes soft enough to purée. You can also pre-cook the sweet potato and store it in the fridge to save time when you actually need it!

2 To prepare the bowl, blend the sweet potato, plant milk, the spices, salt and the coconut milk – giving it an extra creamy consistency. Add plant protein as you like. If you prefer a sweeter taste, add a date.

3 Garnish the bowl with blueberries and enjoy!

Not a banana lover? It's amazing – you will love this creation! The sweet potato is the star of this recipe and takes over all the tasks that a banana usually has. Please don't be put off by the word 'potato' being used in the smoothie bowl chapter. A 'sweet' potato is simply sweeter than you'd expect! Its sugar is absorbed rather slowly by our bodies, which means that blood sugar levels don't risk of going on a rollercoaster ride. Remember: Not all sugars are the same.

NUTRITIONAL VALUES APPROX. 447 KCAL – 6G PROTEIN – 70G CARBOHYDRATES – 10G FIBRE – 16G FAT (5G UNSATURATED)

YOUR DAILY VEGGIES
Smoothie Bowl

about 10 mins

- *50g beetroots (raw or cooked)*
- *1 handful of baby spinach*
- *1/2 avocado*
- *100g frozen berries*
- *2 tsp crushed flaxseeds*
- *1 stoned date (feel free to use more if you like)*
- *100ml plant milk*
- *1 tsp ground Ceylon cinnamon*
- *optional: 10g protein powder (e.g. pea protein)*

TOPPINGS:

- *1 handful of berries, 1/4 peach, bee pollen*

1 Clean and/or peel the vegetables as needed and blend with the frozen berries, crushed flaxseeds, date and plant milk until creamy. Cinnamon also fits very well.

2 You can add protein powder if you like. I like to use pure pea or hemp protein without any additives or flavours.

3 Dress the bowl with berries, a couple of peach slices and bee pollen, but don't limit your creativity!

Voilà. A smoothie bowl that covers your daily dose of vegetables quite well, but doesn't taste like that! I can highly recommend this recipe to anyone who doesn't eat a lot of vegetables (yet) and who therefore prefers to shred and hide them. The beetroot is responsible for the beautiful colour. Beetroots are awesome tubers if you ask me – only very few vegetables can reach the level of vitamins, essential minerals and secondary phytochemicals they contain. They are also said to increase endurance and better your exercise performance! Together with spinach and avocado, we've gathered a vast amount of nutrients to energize us throughout the entire day! And don't forget my praised flaxseeds and their fibres, encouraging digestion and keeping us satisfied for a long time.

NUTRITIONAL VALUES APPROX. 432 KCAL – 8G PROTEIN – 35G CARBOHYDRATES – 18G FIBRE – 27G FAT (21G UNSATURATED)

TURMERIC LATTE
Smoothie Bowl

about 10 mins

- *2–3 thin slices of ginger*
- *100g frozen mango*
- *1 frozen banana*
- *1 tsp oil (preferably flax oil)*
- *250ml plant milk*
- *1/2 tsp ground turmeric*
- *1/2 tsp ground Ceylon cinnamon*
- *pepper*
- *1 pinch of ground cardamom*

TOPPINGS:

- *1/4 banana, bee pollen*

Info

* *Tumeric* 'needs' fat and pepper. The teaspoon of oil in this recipe is needed as turmeric is fat-soluble. This means your body can absorb the spice way better when combined with fat. Black pepper can also significantly increase its usability.

1 Peel the ginger slices and dice them finely. If you are not using organic ginger, make sure to wash it beforehand.

2 Mix the ginger with the frozen mango, frozen banana, oil, plant milk and ground turmeric until creamy.

3 Spices are crucial: to me, cinnamon and pepper are a must. A little bit of cardamom adds the final touch. Mix well in a blender for a second time.

4 Pour the mixture into a bowl and garnish with banana slices and bee pollen.

A Turmeric Latte Smoothie Bowl might not sound as amazing as chocolate ice cream, but to me, it gets pretty close. Spicy and Asian in flavour, combined with a slight sweetness. I'm aware its taste might be hit-or-miss for you, but I can't always please everybody, right? Turmeric is often used as a medicinal plant to slow down ageing and has incredible natural anti-inflammatory properties. That's why it tackles a big variety of illnesses and pains (please find more about turmeric on page 41).

NUTRITIONAL VALUES APPROX. 307 KCAL – 4G PROTEIN – 46G CARBOHYDRATES – 7G FIBRE – 12G FAT (10G UNSATURATED)

Low-Carb BERRY BOWL

about 10 mins

- *150g frozen mixed berries*
- *100ml almond milk*
- *2 tsp almond butter*

TOPPINGS:

- *30g mixed berries, 10g almonds, bee pollen*

1 In a blender, mix the frozen berries, almond milk and almond butter until creamy.

2 Pour into a bowl, garnish with more berries, some almonds and sprinkle with the bee pollen.

This quick smoothie bowl is fruity, super-quick to make and perfect for everyone wanting to reduce calories, carbohydrates and sugars. Berries are among the lightest fruits, only containing about 7g of carbs and sugar as well as about 40 kcal per 100g. Still, they are packed with a huge amount of antioxidants, vitamins and fibre. Thanks to the almond butter, the bowl has a nice creamy texture, without the standard use of bananas. Instead, it benefits from an extra dose of healthy fats and proteins.

Food Swaps: You can swap the almond milk and almond butter for any other kind. Just be creative or use what you already have at home!

Tip

* Depending on your preference, you can add some sweetness. Dates work well, as well as agave and date syrup, honey or simply a piece of banana.

NUTRITIONAL VALUES APPROX. 256 KCAL – 8G PROTEIN – 16G CARBOHYDRATES – 10G FIBRE – 16G FAT (14G UNSATURATED)

PROTEIN CHOCOLATE BOWL –

All-Time Favourite

about 10 mins

- *50g frozen zucchini slices*
- *1/2 banana*
- *150ml coconut water*
- *2 tsp crushed flaxseeds*
- *2 tsp raw, low-fat cocoa powder*
- *2 tbsp hemp protein powder*

TOPPINGS:

- *1/2 banana,*
1 handful of raspberries,
1 tsp grated coconut,
1 tsp cocoa nibs

1 Steamed and then frozen zucchini slices are the base of this bowl. To make these, cut a zucchini in about 2cm-thick slices and steam them for 5–10 minutes in a saucepan or pressure cooker. Spread the slices on paper towels and let them cool. If you have enough space in your freezer, freeze them lying next to each other on a plate so they don't stick to each other. Once they're frozen put them in a bag.

2 To make the bowl, mix the zucchini slices, banana (fresh or frozen), coconut water, flaxseeds, cocoa powder and protein powder. My favourite here is hemp protein. As for the topping, slice the other half of the banana and also dress your bowl with some raspberries, grated coconut and cocoa nibs.

My favourite 'sporty' smoothie bowl. After working out, in the morning or during the day, it provides proteins, large amounts of fibre and is nicely low in carbs. Using the zucchini as the 'invisible' banana creates a creamy texture, is neutral in taste and helps to reduce sugar. And the hemp protein, which usually isn't highly processed, not only offers 45% protein content, but also all the essential amino acids, a lot of fibre and an ideal ratio of omega-3 and omega-6 fatty acids.

Info

* *Coconut water* is Mother Nature's sports drink. It has isotonic properties and balances out the loss of electrolytes when sweating.

NUTRITIONAL VALUES APPROX. 324 KCAL – 15G PROTEIN – 30G CARBOHYDRATES – 18G FIBRE – 13G FAT (6G UNSATURATED)

GREEN SUPERPOWER
Smoothie Bowl

about 10 mins

- *100g frozen zucchini slices*
- *100g frozen mango*
- *1 handful baby spinach*
- *50g avocado*
- *1 stoned date*
- *200ml coconut water*
- *2 tsp hulled hemp seeds*
- *2 tsp powdered wheatgrass*
- *1 tsp powdered spirulina*

TOPPINGS:

- *20g frozen mango, 50g dragon fruit, 1 tsp flaked coconut*

Tip

* An *avocado* is ripe, when it's soft. Pear shaped, longish avocados usually have more pulp and a smaller stone compared to small round avocados. My success ratio is close to 100%!

1 In a blender, mix the frozen zucchini slices that have been previously steamed (see page 107, Protein Chocolate Bowl), with the frozen mango, baby spinach, a big piece of avocado, date and coconut water.

2 For more superpower, add the hulled hemp seeds, wheatgrass and spirulina. Blend again.

3 As a topping, use frozen mango pieces, shape little balls of pink dragon fruit with a small spoon and sprinkle with flaked coconut.

'Green' is usually associated with being healthy, and with this recipe we are living up to this cliché. A concentrated number of ingredients that scream: SUPERPOWERS! Although I am an advocate for natural, whole, unprocessed foods, I occasionally use powdered wheatgrass or spirulina in my dishes. They contain an incredible concentration of nutrients like vitamins, minerals and chlorophyll. Both powders are detoxifying, support the immune system and encourage the production of white and red blood cells. Spirulina is furthermore rich in protein with around 60% in its natural state – without being filtered or having oil extracted!

NUTRITIONAL VALUES APPROX. 419 KCAL – 14G PROTEIN – 47G CARBOHYDRATES – 13G FIBRE – 19G FAT (13G UNSATURATED)

Yum

APPLE PIE
Smoothie Bowl

about 10 mins

- *1 fresh apple*
- *50g plant yoghurt (e.g. cashew or coconut yoghurt)*
- *100ml plant milk*
- *1 tsp nut butter*
- *2 tsp crushed flaxseeds or 2 tsp psyllium husks*
- *1 tsp ground Ceylon cinnamon*
- *grated nutmeg*
- *1/2 tsp ground ginger*
- *1 pinch of salt*

TOPPINGS:

- *20g fruit rawnola, 1 tsp nut butter*

NUTRITIONAL VALUES APPROX.

370 KCAL – 9G PROTEIN – 38G CARBOHYDRATES – 12G FIBRE – 19G FAT (15G UNSATURATED)

1 Wash and core the apple, cut it into slices. I also like to put aside some slices for the topping.

2 Purée the apple with the yoghurt (I like plant-based cashew or coconut yoghurt the best), plant milk and a nut butter of your choice until creamy.

3 To get a thicker texture, I add crushed flaxseeds or psyllium husks. The latter don't stand out at all and you barely notice them when eating! Flaxseeds, on the other hand, add a nutty flavour but are noticeable as tiny seeds in your mouth.

4 For the true 'apple pie' taste, you can't leave out cinnamon and some nutmeg, ginger and salt!

5 Garnish the bowl with homemade Fruit Rawnola (see page 207), apple slices and nut butter.

Apple pie – who doesn't love it? Since we can't have cake for breakfast every day, I had the idea of turning all the flavours of this beloved delightfulness into a smoothie bowl. The basis of this bowl isn't so typical though: no bananas, no frozen fruit – but with fresh apple, some plant yoghurt, the unique swelling properties of seeds and the right spices. Nutmeg, ginger and salt may sound like they will take some time getting used to but please trust me, the spices make the combination of flavours just perfect! Just give it a try!
PS: This recipe is low histamine!

CHOCOLATE-SQUASH
Smoothie Bowl

about 45 mins

- *100g Hokkaido squash*
- *1 frozen banana*
- *1 tsp nut butter*
- *200ml plant milk*
- *1 tsp ground Ceylon cinnamon*
- *1/2 tsp ground ginger*
- *grated nutmeg*
- *2 tsp raw, low-fat cocoa powder*

TOPPINGS:

- *10g dark vegan chocolate, 1 tsp flaked coconut, 1 tsp date syrup*

Tip

* *Cocoa powder* should be raw and without any additives. Processed cocoa and sugar mixtures are not the same!

1 Cut the squash into pieces, remove the seeds and cook for 15 minutes in a pressure cooker until the pieces are soft. You can peel the squash before or after cooking. Briefly purée the squash using a blender – and you'll have homemade squash purée! In the US you can find this ready-made in a can. For this bowl, you let the purée cool down or maybe have it already prepared in your fridge or freezer.

2 Mix the purée with the frozen banana, nut butter (e.g. almond) and a plant milk of your choice. For a certain something I add cinnamon, ginger and some nutmeg. Put aside half of this mixture and add the cocoa powder to the other half, giving it another blend.

3 To create a swirl similar to my picture, take a bowl and pour in both the mixtures simultaneously from opposite sides. Chop dark chocolate and add it to the top of the smoothie bowl with flaked coconut and some date syrup.

Chocolate Squash Pie … once upon a time, I fell in love with such a dessert in America. Inspired by the fact that squashes can be turned into savoury soups or main courses, I wanted to give this vegetable a grand appearance as part of the sweet smoothie bowls. Squashes are not only delicious sides to meat dishes – they are diverse and also shine bright as breakfast creations.

NUTRITIONAL VALUES APPROX. 428 KCAL – 10G PROTEIN – 47G CARBOHYDRATES – 7G FIBRE – 20G FAT (12G UNSATURATED)

SALTED CARAMEL BROWNIE
Smoothie Bowl with Rawnola

about 10 mins

- *1 stoned date*
- *1 frozen banana*
- *150ml plant milk (e.g. almond milk)*
- *2 tsp nut butter (best: hazelnut butter)*
- *2 tsp raw, low-fat cocoa powder*
- *some vanilla powder*
- *1 pinch of salt*
- *1 tsp ground Ceylon cinnamon*

TOPPINGS:

- *20g rawnola, 1/2 banana, 1 tsp nut butter, 1 tsp cocoa nibs*

Info

* I consider *dates* to be among my favourite sweeteners, since they are packed with essential minerals. They also tackle daily stress!

1 In a blender, mix the date, frozen banana, plant milk, nut butter and cocoa powder until creamy.

2 The spices are very important for this recipe, since the caramel flavour is only brought to life once the spices, date and nut butter come together. Hazelnut butter is the best choice, but any other kind will also work. A little bit of vanilla, a good pinch of salt and 1 tsp cinnamon are the perfect combination. Simply add to the puréed mixture and mix everything again.

3 Pour the mixture into a bowl and dress with some home-made Ultimate Rawnola (recipe on page 204), banana slices, nut butter and cocoa nibs.

Are we talking breakfast or dessert here? To this day, I am not entirely sure about that. Surprisingly, this bowl tastes so sinful, my mother – obviously confused – asked me the other day: 'Are you sure this is healthy?' Hard to believe yet true: Yes, it is! I am also repeatedly amazed about how easily, and naturally, you can create a caramel flavour. We are definitely not talking about a 'light' breakfast, but about the perfect bowl for anyone with a sweet tooth!
PS: This recipe was so popular in my German cookbook, that it got added to menus in several restaurants!

NUTRITIONAL VALUES APPROX. 532 KCAL – 11G PROTEIN – 58G CARBOHYDRATES – 11G FIBRE – 26G FAT (21G UNSATURATED)

Lunch & Dinner Bowls

4

I dedicated most of the recipes to the main meal of the day. Whether around noon or in the evening, well-balanced bowls with healthy carbohydrates, proteins and fats provide you with a satisfied feeling and are just waiting to be tried by you! The stars of this chapter are definitely vegetables. They're colourful, diverse and incredibly healthy. There's no room for monotony and dullness on the following pages since you can prepare vegetables in countless different ways. This chapter also offers a lot of vegan dishes!

Classic Fitness Dish:
MINCED BEEF STIR-FRY

about 30 mins

- *50g uncooked rice*
- *(e.g. long grain or brown rice)*
- *salt*
- *100g low-fat minced beef*
- *3 tsp coconut or avocado oil*
- *pepper*
- *chilli powder*
- *100g zucchini*
- *100g canned sweetcorn*
- *1 handful fresh basil*

1 Rinse the rice, cook it with a lot of water and salt according to the package instructions. Drain in a sieve.

2 Brown the minced beef with 1–2 tsp oil and season with salt, pepper and chilli powder. I usually use avocado or coconut oil because these kinds are very heat-stable!

3 Clean and cut the zucchini into small dice. Rinse the sweetcorn with water. As soon as the meat is done, put it aside and sauté the vegetables in the same pan until golden brown. If the vegetables appear dry or hard, I like to add a splash of water to the frying pan!

4 Wash and shake dry the basil, chop it and then add it with the meat to the vegetables. Stir-fry all the ingredients for another 5 minutes and season with some more spices if you like!

This recipe is tied to a lot of positive memories. When I was about 17 years old and just starting to enjoy exercising, the minced beef stir-fry was a common part of my diet. For lunch, dinner or on the go – I focused on building mass and muscles! Today I don't eat meat as frequently anymore, but I am still a fan of this dish. It's also very popular with men!
PS: Prefer a low-carb version? Look for 'konjac' rice! Not super common yet, but definitely worth searching for.

NUTRITIONAL VALUES APPROX. 500 KCAL – 29G PROTEIN – 56G CARBOHYDRATES – 4G FIBRE – 19G FAT (11G UNSATURATED)

Info

* *Rice* may be contaminated with the toxic element 'arsenic', which can cause serious health problems. You can minimize this problem by rinsing the grains thoroughly, cooking them in several litres of water and then draining the rice in a sieve – just like pasta.

ROCKET WITH
Beef Fillet & Pan-Fried Red Radish

1 Clean the red radishes and cut them into quarters. Clean the tomatoes and cut these in half. Wash and shake dry the basil, chop roughly.

2 Wash and drain the rocket in a sieve.

3 Using a sharp knife, cut the beef fillet into long, thin strips. Make sure to cut across the muscle fibres – that's the best way to get a tender result! Sprinkle with the whole peppercorns.

4 For the yoghurt dressing, mix all the ingredients together and season with salt and pepper to taste. Put aside for now.

about 30 mins

FOR THE SALAD:

- *50g red radish*
- *100g small tomatoes*
- *1 handful fresh basil*
- *50g rocket*
- *100g beef fillet*
- *whole peppercorns*
- *1 tbsp pine nuts*
- *2–3 tsp avocado oil*
- *salt*
- *pepper*

FOR THE DRESSING:

- *50g plant yoghurt (e.g. cashew)*
- *30ml plant milk*
- *3 tsp apple cider vinegar or regular vinegar*
- *1 small handful fresh herbs (e.g. basil, chives, parsley)*
- *1 tsp honey*
- *salt*
- *pepper*

Tip

* Not every salad dressing needs to contain oil! Yoghurt dressings especially taste amazing without any added oil and are a great low-calorie alternative.

5 Roast the pine nuts without any fat for about 2 minutes in a frying pan over low heat. Swirl the pan constantly to keep the nuts moving, otherwise they will burn! Put aside.

6 Sauté the red radish, tomatoes and basil with a little avocado oil. The radish should become translucent and the tomatoes soft. Season with salt and pepper.

7 Heat some avocado oil in a frying pan. Once it's hot, place the beef strips into the pan and sear them for a couple of minutes on each side. I can't give you a recommended cooking time for this step – rare, medium or well done? It's your choice!

8 In a bowl, toss the salad with the dressing and place the fried vegetables on top. Add the beef fillet and garnish with some pine nuts.

If I'm eating out and am unsure which dish suits my diet, I often go for a salad with beef strips, which is available in most regular restaurants. Dressing on the side please and preferably just plain vinegar and olive oil. The dressings usually hide cane sugar, saturated fats, cheap oil and artificial flavours … and all of a sudden your 'healthy' salad turns into a sugar and calorie bomb. At home you can simply mix a delicious yoghurt-herb dressing with just a few ingredients. Let's say goodbye to ready-made dressings – at least within our own four walls.

NUTRITIONAL VALUES APPROX. 370KCAL – 28G PROTEIN – 13G CARBOHYDRATES – 4G FIBRE – 22G FAT (13G UNSATURATED)

Classic Fitness Bowl:
CHICKEN & VEGGIE-RICE

about 30 mins

- *100g broccoli*
- *3–4 tsp avocado oil*
- *oregano, fresh or dried*
- *thyme, fresh or dried*
- *salt*
- *pepper*
- *100g chicken breast*
- *100g tomatoes*
- *1 handful fresh basil*
- *1 handful baby spinach*
- *50g avocado*

NUTRITIONAL VALUES APPROX.

388 KCAL – 32G PROTEIN – 13G CARBOHYDRATES – 8G FIBRE – 23G FAT (17G UNSATURATED)

Info

* *Broccoli* contains the powerful antioxidant sulforaphane, which is considered a strong and natural weapon for battling cancer cells! It is not very heat-resistant though, so don't heat up the broccoli-rice for too long or at too high a temperature.

1 Wash the broccoli, cut off the florets and, using a food processor, shred them to create 'rice'. In a frying pan, sauté the broccoli rice with a little avocado oil, oregano, thyme, salt and pepper over low heat. Add a little bit of water and steam the broccoli for about 10 minutes. Make sure the broccoli is only moist, not covered with water. Cover the pan with a lid.

2 Cut the chicken breast in slices and sauté these with a little avocado oil and pepper in a hot frying pan.

3 Clean and cut the tomatoes into small pieces. Wash and shake dry the basil, then chop it. Carefully heat both ingredients with 1 tsp avocado oil, the pepper and oregano in a saucepan. This is a super quick way to create a tomato sauce – it only takes 3–4 minutes!

4 Wash and spin-dry the baby spinach and spread it as the base in a bowl. Cut the avocado in slices and add them together with the broccoli-rice, chicken and tomato sauce.

Low-carb, high in protein and with healthy fats – the fitness classic. The shredded broccoli reminds you of rice while, of course, you're avoiding the calories and carbohydrates. But for some people – including me – broccoli tends to be hard to digest. That's also a reason I prefer to chop it into small pieces. Steaming also helps to prevent a bloated belly!

CURRIED CHICKEN SALAD

with Cashews, Rice & Baby Spinach

1 Preheat the oven to 165°C. Spread the cashews on a baking tray lined with baking parchment and roast for 15 minutes – there is no need for oil.

2 The chicken breast is being poached, not fried. That way, pulling it into pieces will be the easiest! You can either cook it for 20 minutes in a pressure cooker or a normal saucepan. To do this, cover the chicken with water, add salt and pepper and bring to the boil. Then let it simmer over low heat for 20–25 minutes and let it cool afterwards.

about 30 mins

FOR THE SALAD:

- *30g cashew nuts*
- *100g chicken breast*
- *salt*
- *pepper*
- *30g uncooked rice*
- *1 handful baby spinach*
- *spring onions, to taste*
- *1 handful fresh basil*

FOR THE SAUCE:

- *50g yoghurt (e.g. cashew)*
- *1–2 tbsp fresh lemon juice*
- *1–2 tsp honey*
- *1 tsp curry powder*
- *1/2 tsp turmeric powder*
- *salt*
- *pepper*

3 Rinse the rice thoroughly and boil it according to packet instructions in salted water. Wash, clean and spin-dry the spinach.

4 For the sauce, mix the cashew yoghurt, lemon juice, honey, curry powder and turmeric in a bowl. Season with salt and pepper.

5 Clean and cut the spring onions in thin slices. Wash and shake dry the basil, chop finely. Put aside a few whole cashew nuts for the topping. Crush the remaining cashew nuts.

6 Tear the cold chicken into small pieces – I use a fork or simply my fingers. Mix the chicken with the onions, basil, cashew nuts and the sauce.

7 The spinach goes into your bowl first, followed up by your chicken salad, rice and the cashew nuts as a topping!

This dish was quite a surprise for my family, since it's pretty uncommon for me. Usually, I'm not a fan of chicken salads because, with all the mayonnaise and dressing, they tend to be rather heavy on the stomach. Instead, I use cashew yoghurt and transform a classic into a light and healthy dish that to this day everyone has liked. I'd consider this a typical 'men's dish' – or at least a dish my brother would enjoy having cooked for him.

Tip

* The Curried Cashew & Chicken Salad can be stored for 1–2 days in the fridge. This even benefits the overall taste since the flavours start to combine!

NUTRITIONAL VALUES APPROX. 454 KCAL – 34G PROTEIN – 43G CARBOHYDRATES – 4G FIBRE – 17G FAT (13G UNSATURATED)

CHICKEN AVOCADO SALAD
with Sun-Dried Tomatoes & Quinoa

about 30 mins

FOR THE SALAD:

- *50g chicken breast*
- *30g uncooked quinoa*
- *1 handful of salad greens*
- *50g avocado*
- *20g sun-dried tomatoes*
- *50g red radishes*
- *1 dash of fresh lime juice*
- *salt*
- *pepper*
- *chilli powder*
- *1 handful basil*

FOR THE DRESSING:

- *1 small tbsp olive oil*
- *1 tbsp fresh lime juice*
- *1–2 tsp honey*
- *salt*
- *pepper*

1 Cook the chicken breast whole in either a pressure cooker for 20 minutes or a regular saucepan, covered with water, for 25 minutes. Cut it to see if it's fully cooked – if so, let it cool.

2 Using a sieve, rinse the quinoa thoroughly with water. Bring it to the boil in a saucepan with water, reduce the heat and let it simmer for 15 minutes.

3 Wash, clean and spin-dry the salad greens. Dice the avocado and cut the sun-dried tomatoes into small pieces. Clean and cut the radishes into pieces as well. In a bowl, mix the avocado, tomatoes and radishes with the lime juice and mash everything with a fork until you have a finely chopped texture. Season with salt, pepper and chilli powder.

4 Tear the chicken breast with a fork or your fingers. Wash, shake dry and roughly chop the basil. Add both to the avocado mash. For the dressing, stir all the ingredients together and pour it over the greens.

5 Place the salad greens in a bowl, drain the quinoa in a sieve and arrange it together with the chicken avocado salad on the greens.

NUTRITIONAL VALUES APPROX. 378 KCAL – 20G PROTEIN – 30G CARBOHYDRATES – 8G FIBRE – 19G FAT (15G UNSATURATED)

MEAL PREP BOWL

1 Preheat the oven to 180°C. Place the chicken breast in a saucepan, add a little salt and pepper and cover with water. Bring to the boil and then reduce the heat until you are left with a simmer. After around 20 minutes take out the chicken, cut it open and check if the meat is completely done. If so, let it cool down. Alternatively, you can use a pressure cooker.

2 Using a fork, prick holes in the skin of the sweet potato and place the whole potato on a baking tray lined with baking parchment. In the preheated oven, bake the potato for 30–60 minutes, depending on its size. To check, simply pierce the potato with a knife and see if it's soft all around.

about 45 mins

FOR THE BOWL:

- 100g chicken breast
- salt
- pepper
- 200g sweet potato
- 1 egg
- 50g small tomatoes
- 100g zucchini

FOR THE PAPRIKA-TAHINI SAUCE:

- 2 tbsp tahini
- 1 tbsp fresh lemon juice
- 2 tbsp plant milk
- 1 tsp honey
- 1 tsp sweet paprika powder
- salt
- pepper

Tip

* Microwave? Not for me. Just to be safe. Opinions are mixed on this matter but some studies have shown cancer-causing effects and a reduction in nutritional values.

3 Place the whole egg in a saucepan of boiling water and cook for 12 minutes. Only peel the egg just before serving. Wash the tomatoes.

4 Wash and clean the zucchini. Turn the zucchini into noodles by using a spiral vegetable slicer. You can get them in kitchen supply stores and well-stocked supermarkets!

5 For the paprika-tahini sauce, mix together all the ingredients and season with salt and pepper. I prefer to wait until serving before I pour the sauce over the dish.

6 Let all the ingredients cool down completely and store them in the fridge using a lidded container. Before eating, reheat the chicken, sweet potato and zucchini noodles in a saucepan or in the oven. Peel the egg and cut into quarters.

Planning and preparation – that's half the battle, even when it comes to daily meal plans. For people with little time, little patience or a big appetite (that comes out of nowhere and usually ends up in quick and unhealthy choices), I'd strongly recommend storing basic foods readily prepared in the fridge. That's pretty common, especially in the fitness world, and is called 'meal prep'.

NUTRITIONAL VALUES APPROX. 576 KCAL – 40G PROTEIN – 60G CARBOHYDRATES – 11G FIBRE – 19G FAT (15G UNSATURATED)

TURKEY-ZUCCHINI MEATBALLS

with Wild Rice & Curry Sauce

about 45 mins

1 Preheat the oven to 190°C and line a baking tray with baking parchment.

2 Peel the onion, dice finely and sauté in a frying pan with a little avocado oil until translucent. Clean the zucchini and either grate it by hand or shred it using a food processor. Either cut the turkey breast into very fine pieces or use the food processor. Wash the herbs, shake dry and chop.

3 Separate the egg white and yolk. Whisk the egg white with a pinch of salt until stiff. One egg is enough for about 18 meatballs (that's more than one serving).

FOR 3 SERVINGS (EQUALS 18 MEATBALLS):

- *20g onion*
- *avocado oil*
- *200g zucchini*
- *150g turkey breast*
- *2 handfuls fresh herbs (alternatively 3 tsp dried herbs)*
- *1 egg*
- *salt*
- *30g almond or coconut flour*
- *1 dash fresh lemon juice*
- *pepper*
- *sweet paprika*
- *30g uncooked rice (e.g. mixed rice, wild, brown or basmati rice)*
- *50g canned sweetcorn*
- *2 tsp avocado oil*
- *1 handful baby spinach*

FOR THE CURRY SAUCE:

- *50ml creamy coconut milk (about 60% coconut)*
- *1 dash fresh lemon juice*
- *1 tsp date syrup or honey*
- *1/2 tsp curry powder*
- *1 knife tip ground cumin*
- *salt*
- *pepper*

Since I don't like wasting any food, I usually just prepare this amount of meatballs and store them covered in the fridge – or I just cook for my family as well.

4 In a bowl, mix the zucchini, onion, flour, lemon juice and herbs. Season. From my experience, the meatballs need a lot of pepper, ground paprika and salt.

5 Work the turkey and egg yolk into the mixture. As the last ingredient, fold in the stiff egg white. Using a spoon or wetted hands, form the meatballs and place them on the prepared baking tray. Bake for 25–30 minutes in the pre-heated oven.

6 Rinse the rice, cook it with a lot of water and some salt according to the package instructions. Drain in a sieve.

7 Rinse the canned sweetcorn with water and continue by stir-frying it with a little avocado oil in a frying pan. This should only take a couple of minutes!

8 For the curry sauce, simply mix all the ingredients together and season with salt and pepper.

9 Clean, rinse and spin-dry the baby spinach. Arrange it in a bowl. Place the rice, the meatballs and sweetcorn on top. The sauce tastes great with the spinach or as a dip for the meatballs!

NUTRITIONAL VALUES APPROX. 464 KCAL – 26G PROTEIN – 42G CARBOHYDRATES – 7G FIBRE – 22G FAT (9G UNSATURATED)

TERIYAKI CHICKEN BOWL – *Made by my Brother*

about 30 mins

- *70g uncooked basmati rice*
- *salt*
- *130g chicken breast*
- *75ml teriyaki sauce*
- *2 tsp sesame oil*
- *50g avocado*
- *20g wakame salad*
- *15g pickled pink ginger*

TOPPINGS:

- *10g mayo, 1 tsp roasted black sesame seeds, spring onion*

TERIYAKI SAUCE (HOMEMADE AND REDUCED SUGAR):

- *40ml mild soy sauce*
- *40ml sake*
- *40ml mirin*

Tip

* With this bowl, I like to have Vietnamese slaw as a side!

1 Rinse the rice, cook it with a lot of water and some salt according to the package instructions. Drain in a sieve.

2 For the teriyaki sauce, bring all the ingredients to the boil in a saucepan. Let the sauce reduce for the next 4 minutes while keeping the heat just high enough to produce a foam. You can also use ready-made teriyaki sauce as an alternative – but only when Pamela isn't watching!

3 Cut the chicken breast into strips and marinate the chicken in the teriyaki sauce for 15 minutes. Then, take the strips from the sauce and sear them in a frying pan with some sesame oil. Pour the remaining teriyaki sauce into the frying pan as well and stir-fry until the sauce caramelizes.

4 Slice the avocado. Place the rice into a bowl. Put the chicken strips with the sauce, avocado, wakame salad and pickled ginger onto the rice. Dress with the mayo, sesame seeds and finely chopped spring onions.

Thanks to a vote by my followers, my brother Dennis was asked to contribute a recipe to my book as well! Dennis: 'In contrast to most of Pam's dishes, I am using ready-made products like mayo. I guess it's okay if I break ranks though. I've decided to show you my favourite soul food bowl that always leaves me with a great feeling of satisfaction – thanks to a lot of sauce and mayo.'

NUTRITIONAL VALUES APPROX. 750 KCAL – 44G PROTEIN – 70G CARBOHYDRATES – 4G FIBRE – 30G FAT (22G UNSATURATED)

SWEET SALAD

with Cinnamon-Baked Sweet Potato, Feta & Cinnamon-Date Dressing

about 25 mins

FOR THE SALAD:

- *50g sweet potato*
- *1 tsp coconut oil*
- *1 tsp ground Ceylon cinnamon*
- *1 small pear*
- *1 stoned date*
- *30g feta cheese*
- *20g pecan nuts*
- *50g mixed salad greens*

FOR THE DRESSING:

- *1 tbsp apple cider vinegar or lemon juice*
- *1 tbsp date syrup or 1 stoned date*
- *30ml plant milk (e.g. almond milk)*
- *1/2 tsp ground Ceylon cinnamon*
- *some ground cardamom*
- *pepper*

Info

** Cinnamon is not always the same! Compared to real Ceylon cinnamon, the more affordable Chinese or cassia cinnamon contains more coumarin which, consumed in higher dosages, can harm the liver!*

1 Preheat the oven to 180°C. Peel and dice the sweet potato. Put it into a bowl, add a little coconut oil, sprinkle over some cinnamon and mix until the potato is evenly coated. Then, put it on a baking tray lined with baking parchment and bake in the oven for 20 minutes.

2 Clean and slice the pear. Finely chop the date. Crumble the feta cheese and roughly break the pecan nuts.

3 Wash and shake dry the salad greens. To prepare the cinnamon-date dressing you only need to mix the listed ingredients thoroughly. Taste and add some more of the seasonings if needed.

4 In a big bowl, toss the salad with the dressing and add the sweet potato, fruit, feta cheese and nuts.

Salads don't need to be boring! Sweet, salty, crunchy and creamy – this salad combines them all. Baked sweet potato, juicy pear, sweet dates, some salty feta and a couple of crunchy pecan nuts rounded off by a hint of cinnamon. This dish leaves nothing to be desired!

Food Swaps: A very flexible recipe! Apple works well instead of the pear, dates can be substituted for raisins and pecans with walnuts!

NUTRITIONAL VALUES APPROX. 475 KCAL – 9G PROTEIN – 50G CARBOHYDRATES – 10G FIBRE – 27G FAT (16G UNSATURATED)

VEGGIE PIE –
My Favourite

about 50 mins

- *100g Hokkaido squash*
- *salt*
- *30g uncooked quinoa*
- *50g carrot*
- *50g zucchini*
- *50g mushrooms*
- *1 handful baby spinach*
- *1 handful fresh herbs (e.g. parsley, basil and thyme, alternatively 3 tsp dried herbs)*
- *1 egg*
- *50g peas (fresh of frozen)*
- *chilli powder*
- *grated nutmeg*
- *pepper*
- *1 tsp avocado oil*

TOPPINGS OF CHOICE:

- *Sunflower seeds, vegetable slices*

...Food Swaps...

* You can experiment with all sorts of vegetables and your squash purée can also be made with sweet potatoes! This will taste slightly sweeter, so maybe add an extra pinch of salt.

1 Preheat the oven to 180°C. Peel the squash, remove the seeds and cut into pieces. Cook it in a saucepan with salted water until it's soft, or steam it in a pressure cooker, for about 10 minutes.

2 Rinse the quinoa in a sieve under running water and then cook for 12–15 minutes with a pinch of salt and 2.5 times the volume of water. In the meantime, wash, clean and peel the carrot, zucchini and mushrooms as necessary. Either finely chop everything with a knife or use your food processor. Wash, clean, spin-dry and tear the spinach in smaller pieces. Wash, shake dry and finely chop the fresh herbs.

3 Separate the egg and beat the egg white with a pinch of salt until stiff. The squash pieces should be soft by now – drain and purée them. In a bowl, mix the squash purée, quinoa, carrot and zucchini pieces, spinach, herbs, mushrooms and peas. Season with the salt, pepper and spices, then thoroughly stir in the egg yolk. At last, carefully fold in the beaten egg white.

4 Grease an ovenproof dish with the avocado oil and pour in the mixture. Add the toppings – I love using sunflower seeds and some vegetable slices! Bake for 25–30 minutes and enjoy directly from the dish!

This is one of my absolute favourite recipes! I created it as the very last one and I'm sure it's like the icing on the cake for my cookbook.

NUTRITIONAL VALUES APPROX. 372 KCAL – 21G PROTEIN – 45G CARBOHYDRATES – 9G FIBRE – 11G FAT (7G UNSATURATED)

'Eating enough protein as a vegan? That's only possible with substitutes like tofu, tempeh or protein powder.' Nonsense! Here's a bowl with 100% natural ingredients and over 20g of protein. That roughly equals a protein shake. The amino acids of the foods are either 'complete' proteins right away, or they add up to be 'whole' – just like the protein from a piece of meat. You can find more information on whole plant-based protein sources on page 50.

Vegan Protein BUDDHA BOWL

about 25 mins

FOR THE BOWL:

- *50g uncooked quinoa*
- *salt*
- *50g fine green beans*
- *2–3 tsp avocado oil*
- *pepper*
- *50g mushrooms*
- *30g canned chickpeas*
- *1 tsp sesame seeds*
- *30g baby spinach*

FOR THE PINK HUMMUS:

- *30g canned chickpeas*
- *10g beetroot*
- *1 tsp tahini*
- *1 tsp olive oil or 1 tsp plant milk*
- *1 splash of lemon juice*
- *ground cumin*
- *salt*
- *pepper*

TOPPINGS:

- *10g pumpkin seeds, 10g peeled hemp seeds*

1 Rinse the quinoa in a sieve under running water and cook for 12–15 minutes with a pinch of salt and 2.5 the volume of water.

2 Wash the fine green beans, trim the ends and cut in half. Gently heat the beans in a frying pan with a little avocado oil, salt and pepper. Then deglaze them by pouring in a glass of water and steam by covering with a lid.

3 In the meantime, clean the mushrooms, cut them in slices and toss in with the beans. Steam both for about 3 minutes.

4 Rinse the chickpeas thoroughly under running water using a sieve, drain and then brown them in a frying pan with sesame seeds and avocado oil.

5 For the pink hummus, purée all the ingredients until creamy. Clean, wash and spin-dry the baby spinach and place it in your bowl as a base.

6 Drain the quinoa using a sieve. Place the vegetables, chickpeas and quinoa on the baby spinach. Dress with the pumpkin and hemp seeds and – my favourite part – top with the pink hummus. PS: Check my other hummus versions on page 216!

NUTRITIONAL VALUES APPROX. 564 KCAL – 25G PROTEIN – 45G CARBOHYDRATES – 11G FIBRE – 30G FAT (28G UNSATURATED)

CREAMY ONE-POT RISOTTO

For a risotto you can use all kinds of vegetables! If you are missing an ingredient, simply substitute one vegetable for another or leave it out.

1 Peel the squash and remove the seeds. Cut it into pieces. In a saucepan, sauté with some oil, salt and pepper. After a couple of minutes, add a splash of water and continue sautéing.

2 Meanwhile, clean and cut the vegetables that require a longer cooking time – for example, broccoli, cauliflower or carrots – into pieces. Add them to the squash and check if another splash of water is needed.

3 Clean the mushrooms and cut them into slices. Wash the parsley, shake it dry and chop roughly. Add both to the vegetables in the saucepan, continue heating and season with salt and pepper.

about 45 mins

- *100g Hokkaido squash*
- *2 tsp avocado or coconut oil*
- *salt*
- *pepper*
- *50g broccoli, cauliflower or carrots*
- *50g mushrooms*
- *1 handful fresh parsley*
- *50g uncooked brown rice*
- *50g peas (frozen)*

TOPPINGS:

- *20 g peanuts*

NUTRITIONAL VALUES APPROX.

516 KCAL – 17G PROTEIN – 65G CARBOHYDRATES – 9G FIBRE – 21G FAT (16G UNSATURATED)

Tip

* Perfect for using up all kinds of vegetables! For this recipe, the vegetables don't even need to be fresh and crisp anymore.

4 Rinse the uncooked rice thoroughly and stir it into the vegetables so it can combine with all the different flavours. Don't add any water yet.

5 In the meantime, bring water to the boil in a kettle. Pour boiling water into the saucepan so that the vegetables and rice are half-covered.

6 Let this simmer over medium heat and, as soon as the water is absorbed, add further splashes of hot water.

7 Stirring regularly is key at this point – it is the only way for the risotto to become rich and creamy.

8 Once the rice is al dente, add the remaining vegetables that only require a short cooking time, e.g. frozen peas.

9 Usually, the rice takes about 20–30 minutes to be done. Stir regularly and continue to add water.

10 In the end, all of the liquid should be soaked up and you should be able to scoop the risotto directly from the saucepan. Check if it needs some more seasoning. Once it's done, dress with some peanuts and serve.

Rich, filling and incredibly creamy. So creamy, you might think you've actually used cream. This texture is only made possible by the method of stirring constantly and only adding water splash by splash – which I admit, is not the quickest and easiest way of cooking risotto. On the other hand you are saving time, since you only need a single saucepan and don't need much time to clean up afterwards!

Ayurvedic Detox Bowl – MUNG QUINOA KHICHDI

about 45 mins
+ soaking min. 8 hrs.

- *50g uncooked mung beans*
- *2–3 slices fresh ginger*
- *1/2 tsp turmeric powder*
- *1/2 tsp ground cumin*
- *1/4 tsp ground cardamom*
- *pepper*
- *1/2 tsp Ceylon cinnamon powder*
- *1 tsp coconut oil or ghee*
- *30g uncooked quinoa*
- *50g carrots*
- *50g zucchini*
- *50g fennel*
- *1 small handful fresh parsley*
- *salt*

Info

* Ayurveda? That's a traditional Indian art of healing, and better known as a natural detoxification procedure in the Western world.

1 Soak the mung beans in water – overnight or for at least 8 hours. Afterwards, rinse thoroughly.

2 Peel the ginger slices and chop very finely. Place the ginger in a saucepan, add the spices and some coconut oil or ghee, then lightly sauté until they start to smell nicely.

3 Rinse the quinoa under running water in a sieve and let it drain. Add both the quinoa and mung beans to the saucepan with the spices and sauté for 2–3 minutes. Deglaze with 400ml water and let everything simmer over low heat.

4 Wash and clean the carrots, zucchini and fennel. Peel if needed. Finely dice all three. Wash, shake-dry and chop the parsley. Add everything to the saucepan and let it simmer until the mung beans are done (this will take 20–30 minutes). The water should also be absorbed at the end. Take a taste test, season with salt and pepper if necessary and serve in a bowl.

My favourite Ayurvedic dish with a relaxing and cleansing effect. Our digestion is usually overworked – a light and wholesome dish like khichdi can work miracles in this case. It relieves the digestive tract, heals the intestinal walls and supports the metabolism to ease and detoxify!

NUTRITIONAL VALUES APPROX. 344 KCAL – 18G PROTEIN – 45G CARBOHYDRATES – 14G FIBRE – 7G FAT (2G UNSATURATED)

VEGAN VEGGIE FRITTERS

with Squash, Mushrooms & Quinoa

about 50 mins

1 Peel the squash, remove the seeds, cut it into pieces and steam in a pressure cooker – it only takes 10 minutes to become soft. Alternatively, cook for 15–20 minutes in a regular saucepan with water. Rinse the quinoa in a sieve under running water and then cook for 12–15 minutes with a pinch of salt and 2.5 the volume of water.

2 For the fritters, clean and – if needed – peel the vegetables. Grate the carrots by hand or use a food processor. Finely dice the mushrooms, saving a few slices for the topping.

FOR THE BOWL:

- *30g uncooked quinoa*
- *salt*
- *50g salad greens*
- *1 handful small tomatoes*

FOR THE FRITTERS (MAKES ABOUT 6):

- *150g Hokkaido squash*
- *100g carrots*
- *100g mushrooms (e.g. button mushrooms)*
- *1 handful parsley*
- *salt and pepper*
- *chilli powder*
- *30g oats*
- *2 tbsp peeled hemp seeds*
- *ground cumin*
- *3–4 tsp avocado oil*

FOR THE DRESSING:

- *1 tbsp lemon juice*
- *1 tbsp olive oil*
- *salt and pepper*

NUTRITIONAL VALUES APPROX.

689 KCAL – 21G PROTEIN – 69G CARBOHYDRATES – 14G FIBRE – 34G FAT (27G UNSATURATED)

Tip

* To create a vegetarian variation, add 1 egg to the batter. A nice side effect is that the fritters stay in shape a lot better!

3 Wash, shake dry and roughly chop the parsley. Steam the parsley with the carrots, mushrooms, salt, pepper, a little chilli powder and a splash of water in a saucepan for 5 minutes. When done, there shouldn't be any water left in the saucepan but if there is, just drain it.

4 Remove the squash from the saucepan and purée. Then, toss in the steamed vegetables, oats and hemp seeds. Stir and mash with a fork until you end up with a thick, even consistency. Season with salt, pepper and cumin.

5 Preheat the oven to 150°C. Now, using a spoon, shape little fritters from the batter and brown them on both sides with a little avocado oil in a frying pan. It can be quite a challenge to keep the fritters in shape and not have them fall apart. As a quick fix, stir an additional spoon of oats or flour into the mixture. Also, pushing them back together with the spatula is perfectly fine, because the issue will be solved in the next step anyway.

6 Place the fritters on a baking tray lined with baking parchment and bake them in the preheated oven for 20 minutes. Baking removes the moisture, resulting in a more crispy and firm end result.

7 For the dressing, simply mix together all the ingredients. Clean, wash and spin-dry the salad greens – they go into your bowl first. Wash and add the tomatoes, drizzle the dressing on top. Drain the quinoa using a sieve and place it with the squash fritters on top of the salad. Don't forget the mushroom slices – and enjoy!

Vegan burger patties, fritters or sticks – ready-made, packaged and found in the refrigerated section in organic supermarkets. Well, most of them tend to taste similar and if you take a closer look they are usually produced with a lot of soy and inexpensive oils. The squash-mushroom fritters here are made of high-value ingredients: squash as a foundation, mushrooms add a meaty bite, oats and hemp seeds keep everything together.

VEGAN BURGER PATTIES
with Fries & a Cashew Dip

about 1 h.
+ soaking min. 2 hrs.

FOR THE CASHEW DIP:

- *50g cashews*
- *1 tbsp fresh lemon juice*
- *salt*

FOR THE BURGER PATTIES (MAKE 5 PATTIES):

- *100g sweet potato*
- *50g uncooked lentils*
- *salt*
- *40ml plant milk*
- *1 tbsp sunflower seeds*
- *30g oats*
- *chilli powder*
- *ground cumin*
- *pepper*
- *2-3 tsp avocado oil*

FOR THE FRIES:

- *200g potatoes*
- *1 tsp avocado oil*

▶

1 For the cashew dip, soak the cashew nuts in water – for a minimum of 2 hours; overnight is even better.

2 As the base ingredient for the burger patty I use a small sweet potato. Cook it unpeeled for 15–20 minutes, or if using a pressure cooker, for 10–15 minutes. Peel it afterwards.

3 In the meantime, rinse the lentils under running water in a sieve and continue by cooking them in salted water. The cooking time varies depending on what kind of lentils you are using – in my case, the red ones take around 15 minutes. Drain and set aside.

4 Preheat the oven to 190°C. Wash and clean the potatoes, then cut into strips. Coat them in some avocado oil and season with salt, pepper and cumin. Place on a baking tray lined with baking parchment and bake for 30 minutes until crisp.

5 Purée the cooked sweet potato with some plant milk until creamy. Stir in the lentils, sunflower seeds and oats. Season the burger mixture with the salt, pepper and spices. Shape five patties from the mixture and brown them on both sides in a frying pan with a little avocado oil. Then, place the patties next to the fries in the oven and bake for another 10–15 minutes.

6 Wash and clean the fine green beans, put them into the oven at about the same time as the patties. You don't need to add anything to them. Meanwhile, rinse the cashews under running water, then throw them in a blender. Purée with the fresh lemon ▶

- *salt and pepper*
- *ground cumin*
- *sweet paprika*

FOR THE BOWL:

- *50g fine green beans*
- *50g lettuce*

Tip

* If the patty mixture doesn't stay in shape while frying, adding 1 tbsp of flour can help!

juice, 30ml water and a good pinch of salt. It might take some minutes until the dip is smooth and creamy! To help, simply push the cream back towards the blade so that everything gets puréed evenly.

7 Wash, clean and spin-dry the lettuce. Place it in a bowl and add the fine green beans. Put the burger patties and fries on top and serve the cashew dip on the side.

Burger patties without any meat? Even the men at home will like them. I would recommend this dish to anyone who still need to be convinced about healthy eating. Our sinful pleasures like burgers and fries actually do exist as healthy versions, too. And not only that – they even taste great!

Food Swaps: A bit too high in calories for you? Swap the Cashew Dip with Tomato Sauce and you'll save about 250kcal!

NUTRITIONAL VALUES APPROX. 1.037 KCAL – 34G PROTEIN – 124G CARBOHYDRATES – 17G FIBRE – 44G FAT (36G UNSATURATED)

FROM ABOVE AND BELOW GROUND –

Baked Beetroot, Sweet Potato Fries & Baked Apple

1 Preheat the oven to 180°C.

2 Clean and peel the sweet potatoes and cut into long, slim strips. Add the strips to a bowl with 2 tsp of the avocado oil and toss to coat them evenly. Mix together the seasonings, sprinkle the mixture over the potatoes and toss again. I like to use cumin, salt and pepper.

3 Dice the beetroot – I'd recommend using a paper towel when touching the beetroot, so your fingers won't stain red. Toss the dice in the remaining avocado oil and pepper as well.

about 40 mins

FOR THE VEGETABLES:

- *200g sweet potatoes*
- *3 tsp avocado oil*
- *ground cumin*
- *salt*
- *pepper*
- *100g raw beetroot*
- *100g carrots*
- *100g zucchini*
- *50g red radishes*
- *50g apple*
- *cress*

FOR THE PUMPKIN SEED SAUCE:

- *30ml creamy coconut milk*
- *2 tsp pumpkin seed butter (alternative: tahini)*
- *1 tsp apple cider vinegar or vinegar of your choice*
- *salt*
- *pepper*

Food Swaps

* Parsnips, Jerusalem artichokes, parsley roots or fennel can be integrated into this dish as well! Handle these just like the beetroots.

4 Spread the sweet potato fries and beetroot dice on a baking tray lined with baking parchment and bake for 25–30 minutes. Take everything out of the oven as soon as the fries have turned brown and crispy.

5 In the meantime, clean and peel the carrots and either grate them by hand or use a food processor. Wash and clean the zucchini, turn it into noodles (also called zoodles) using a spiral vegetable slicer. Wash and quarter the radishes.

6 Wash, clean and cut the apple into slices. Place it in the oven as well. Since it only takes around 15 minutes, the timing should be about right.

7 For the pumpkin seed sauce, simply throw all the ingredients into a blender and purée until creamy and smooth. Pour over the zucchini and toss.

8 Put the zucchini into a bowl, place the grated carrot on top of them and, as the next layer, everything from the oven. Lastly, top with the radish and cress.

What do sweet potatoes, beetroot, carrots and radishes all have in common? They grow beneath the earth and, as the plants' roots, they have the job of storing everything the plant needs to live. Baked or raw, shredded or whole – they are super versatile, nutritious and therefore have a regular spot in my diet!

NUTRITIONAL VALUES APPROX. 567 KCAL – 11G PROTEIN – 76G CARBOHYDRATES – 15G FIBRE – 23G FAT (9G UNSATURATED)

Easy, healthy and tastes like there's more work going on than is actually required. Veggies from the oven are perfect for anyone who does not want to stay in the kitchen for 20 minutes straight – just throw the veggies into the oven and set your timer! My favourite way to cook on busy days!

OVEN VEGGIES
with Roasted Chickpeas & Pesto Spinach

about 45 mins

- *30g Spinach, Walnut & Olive Pesto (Recipe on page 215)*
- *100g carrots*
- *150g zucchini*
- *100g mushrooms*
- *150g tomatoes*
- *2–3 tsp avocado oil*
- *2 tsp ground ginger*
- *salt*
- *pepper*
- *30g canned chickpeas*
- *30g baby spinach*
- *optional: dried oregano, chilli powder, dried thyme*

NUTRITIONAL VALUES APPROX.

351 KCAL – 11G PROTEIN – 27G CARBOHYDRATES – 11G FIBRE – 21G FAT (17G UNSATURATED)

1 Preheat the oven to 190°C and prepare the Spinach, Walnut & Olive Pesto.

2 Wash and clean the vegetables and – if needed – peel. If your carrots are on the skinny side, you can use them whole – otherwise cut them in half. Cut the zucchini and mushrooms in slices and the tomatoes in half.

3 Now, drizzle the vegetables with a little avocado oil and season. I like to use ground ginger for the carrots, oregano and chilli powder for both the tomatoes and zucchini and thyme goes well with the mushrooms. An easy alternative: salt and pepper – they go with everything.

4 Rinse the chickpeas thoroughly under running water and let them drain before adding them to a bowl and giving them a toss with ground ginger.

5 Line a baking tray with baking parchment. Place the vegetables and chickpeas on it, spreading them out evenly. Bake for 20–25 minutes in the preheated oven until everything is well done and looks deliciously brown.

6 In the meantime clean, wash and spin-dry the baby spinach and mix it with the homemade pesto. The spinach goes into your bowl first, followed up by the veggies from the oven and some more pesto.

SPAGHETTI
with Vegan Lentil Bolognese

1 Optional: peel and chop the onions, sauté them with a little avocado oil until translucent.

2 Wash, clean and – if necessary – peel the carrots, mushrooms and pepper. Then, either mince them very finely by hand using a knife or shred them in a food processor. Cut the olives in slices. Wash, shake dry and chop the herbs.

3 Sauté the vegetables with herbs, salt, seasonings and 1 tsp avocado oil for around 5 minutes. If you are using fresh herbs, take a handful – for example a mixture of rosemary, parsley and basil. If it's dried herbs – 1 tsp each.

about 25 mins

SERVES 2
(350G BOLOGNESE)

- *50g carrots*
- *50g mushrooms*
- *50g pepper*
- *20g olives*
- *1 handful fresh herbs (e.g. basil, rosemary)*
- *salt, pepper*
- *chilli powder to taste*
- *2–3 tsp avocado oil*
- *25g uncooked lentils (e.g. red lentils)*
- *200g tomato passata*
- *80g uncooked spaghetti (e.g. made from legumes, rice or wholegrain spelt)*
- *optional: onions, some avocado oil*

TOPPINGS:

- *2 tsp yeast flakes*

Tip

* Stored in an air-tight container in the fridge, the Bolognese sauce is good for a couple of days. And make sure to combine it with various other dishes! For example, with the zoodles from page 157.

4 Rinse the lentils under running water using a sieve and let them drain. In a saucepan, bring them to a simmer with the tomato passata, 150ml water and your vegetables. Stir constantly. Depending on what kind of lentils you are using, the cooking time varies – red lentils take around 15 minutes. When done, have a taste and season if necessary.

5 Meanwhile, cook your favourite pasta according to the package instructions in salted water and drain when done. I also love to quickly stir-fry the pasta in avocado oil.

6 Top the pasta with the Bolognese sauce and serve. How about some Parmesan cheese? The vegan alternative is nutritional yeast flakes!

Is this healthy? Sure! Let's start with the Bolognese sauce: Once you've tasted this one, you won't feel the need to include meat anymore. That's even been approved by my dad! Diced vegetables, lentils and (most importantly) the right choice of herbs make all the difference. And also for the pasta: there's no need to choose the classic low-nutrient white wheat pasta. These days you can choose from wholegrain, spelt or even pasta made from chickpeas, beans or lentils. They are gluten-free and even offer a much higher protein content! In this picture for this you can see spaghetti made from chickpeas and brown rice flour. It was super delicious!
PS: My brother Dennis likes to add 2–3x the amount of olives!

NUTRITIONAL VALUES APPROX. 460 KCAL – 22G PROTEIN – 62G CARBOHYDRATES – 10G FIBRE – 14G FAT (8G UNSATURATED)

Light Zucchini Noodles with
VEGAN LENTIL BOLOGNESE

about 50 mins

- *1 serving Vegan Lentil Bolognese (recipe on page 154)*
- *20g uncooked lentils*
- *salt*
- *100g zucchini*
- *50g mushrooms*
- *pepper*
- *50g spinach*
- *grated nutmeg*
- *50g artichoke hearts*

NUTRITIONAL VALUES APPROX.

340 KCAL – 16G PROTEIN – 34G CARBOHYDRATES – 7G FIBRE – 15G FAT (12G UNSATURATED)

1 Cook the Vegan Bolognese (see recipe on page 154). You can prepare it fresh or use some you made earlier and have stored in the fridge. Rinse the lentils under running water using a sieve, then cook them in boiling, salted water. The lentils could be pre-cooked and stored in the fridge as well.

2 Wash and clean the zucchini then turn them into zoodles with a spiral vegetable slicer. Mix the zoodles with the Bolognese sauce and heat the mix on the stove until the noodles turn soft. This will usually take 5–10 minutes.

3 Clean the mushrooms, cut them in slices and braise them lightly with salt, pepper and a splash of water in a frying pan.

4 Wash and clean the spinach, then wilt it by briefly by heating it up with a splash of water in a covered frying pan. Season with salt, pepper and nutmeg to your taste.

5 Chop the artichokes. Place the lentils, Bolognese-zoodles, spinach and mushrooms in a bowl, top with the artichokes. Et voilà – a quick and simple dish!

Feeling like a light dish today? Sometimes there's no need for a 'whole', highly nutritious meal – because you might still feel full after your plate of spaghetti with the Vegan Lentil Bolognese (page 154). This vegetable bowl is prepared in no time, combines delicious and savoury flavours and is very easy on your stomach. And yes, I do know zoodles aren't 'real' noodles. They are not trying to be that anyway. I just consider them a variation in how I serve my vegetables.

QUICK PESTO SALAD
with Zucchini & Roasted Walnuts

about 25 mins

- *50g Spinach, Walnut & Olive Pesto (Recipe page 215)*
- *20g walnuts*
- *200g zucchini*
- *100g small tomatoes*
- *20g olives*
- *1 handful baby spinach*

NUTRITIONAL VALUES APPROX.

397 KCAL – 10G PROTEIN – 14G CARBOHYDRATES – 5G FIBRE – 34G FAT (28G UNSATURATED)

Tip

* Not into a cold salad today? Just heat the ingredients in a frying pan after step 4. Zucchini and pesto are just as delicious served as a hot meal.

1 Preheat the oven to 165°C. Prepare the Spinach, Walnut & Olive Pesto (see recipe on page 215). You can prepare it fresh or already have some stored in your fridge.

2 Place the walnuts on a baking tray and roast them for 10 minutes. Turn each nut after 5 minutes. And oh – there's no need for oil!

3 Clean and wash the zucchini, then, using a spiral vegetable slicer, turn them into zoodles. Wash, clean and cut the tomatoes in halves. Slice the olives. For the baby spinach: wash, clean, spin-dry and tear it, making the pieces a little smaller.

4 Mix the zoodles with the pesto in a bowl and add the remaining ingredients – the easiest way is to use your hands. Roughly break the walnuts apart, putting two whole ones aside for the topping.

5 You can serve the dish right away or store it for up to 2 days in the fridge.

A bowl I could cook almost every single day … well 'cooking' might be an exaggeration here. Since the main ingredients stay raw, you should be done in the blink of an eye. It works well as a meal prep dish or for on the go. The zucchini stays firm and a pesto dressing doesn't leak. Only the roasted nuts shouldn't be added until just before enjoying this dish!

QUINOA SALAD –
The Classic

about 20 mins

FOR THE SALAD:

- *50g uncooked quinoa*
- *salt*
- *50g cucumber*
- *50g small tomatoes*
- *50g radishes*
- *50g avocado*
- *30g red cabbage*
- *1 handful lettuce*
- *1 handful fresh parsley*

FOR THE DRESSING:

- *1 tbsp lemon juice or vinegar*
- *1 tbsp olive, flaxseed or hemp oil*
- *2 tbsp plant milk*
- *1–2 tsp agave syrup*
- *salt and pepper*

TOPPINGS:

- *10g pumpkin seeds*

Tip

* *Quinoa* protects itself from pests with saponin, a substance that is also responsible for the slightly bitter taste. If you rinse your quinoa thoroughly you can reduce that issue!

1 Rinse the quinoa in a sieve and cook with 2.5 the volume of water and a pinch of salt for 12–15 minutes, until all the water has been absorbed.

2 In the meantime, wash, clean, peel if needed and dice the vegetables. With the listed ingredients you can see the kinds of veggies I like the most for my quinoa salad. But if you can find something else in your kitchen – just toss it in there as well! Wash and spin-dry both the lettuce and parsley, tear them roughly.

3 Put some paper towels on a big plate and scoop the quinoa onto it. The bigger the surface, the quicker it cools down.

4 Mix the liquid ingredients for the dressing, season with salt and pepper. As soon as the quinoa is lukewarm or cold, mix with veggies, lettuce and parsley and pour over the dressing. Top with the pumpkin seeds.

Quinoa is sometimes called 'the Inca's gold' … for a good reason! These little grains are probably my favourite plant-based source of protein because they contain all the essential amino fatty acids, which means they form a 'complete' protein. This pseudo-cereal is gluten-free and, compared to our usual grains, quinoa offers a lot more vitamins and minerals.

NUTRITIONAL VALUES APPROX. 484 KCAL – 15G PROTEIN – 42G CARBOHYDRATES – 9G FIBRE – 27G FAT (22G UNSATURATED)

FRUITY QUINOA SALAD – *A New Interpretation*

about 20 mins

FOR THE SALAD:

- *50g uncooked quinoa*
- *1 pinch of salt*
- *50g canned chickpeas*
- *1/2 apple*
- *20g grapes*
- *20g blueberries*
- *20g goji berries*
- *20g almonds*
- *1 handful lettuce*

FOR THE DRESSING:

- *1/2 apple*
- *1 tbsp fresh lemon juice*
- *30ml plant milk (e.g. almond milk)*
- *1/2 tsp ground Ceylon cinnamon*
- *salt and pepper*

NUTRITIONAL VALUES APPROX.

510 KCAL – 19G PROTEIN – 75G CARBOHYDRATES – 20G FIBRE – 16G FAT (14G UNSATURATED)

1 Rinse the quinoa in a sieve and cook with 2.5 times the volume of water and a pinch of salt for 12–15 minutes, until all the water has been absorbed. Put some paper towels on a big plate and scoop the quinoa onto it so it can cool down.

2 In the meantime, rinse the chickpeas under running water. Let them drain and continue with roasting them in a frying pan – no oil needed – until they're golden brown.

3 Wash and clean the fruits, cut up the bigger kinds if needed. I love to use half an apple, grapes and some berries. Dried fruit like goji berries work great as well! Roughly chop the almonds. Wash, clean and spin-dry the lettuce, then tear it into smaller pieces.

4 For the dressing, mix all the listed ingredients in a blender. Season with salt and pepper to your taste.

5 Now mix the quinoa with the fruits, lettuce, roasted chickpeas and chopped almonds. Finally, pour over the dressing and give everything another toss. Serve in a bowl and enjoy!

I love quinoa salads so much, I couldn't just leave it with the veggie version (page 161). Quinoa even tastes super delicious combined with sweet, fruity flavours. You can replace or add further ingredients as you like, there's really no right or wrong. I do have a rule of thumb though: one sweet fruit (grapes), one crispy fruit (apple), something savoury (chickpeas) and something with crunch (almonds).

RAW RAINBOW BOWL
with Mango Dressing

about 20 mins

FOR THE BOWL:

- *1 handful lettuce*
- *50g zucchini*
- *50g carrot*
- *50g beetroot*
- *50g radishes*
- *50g cucumber*
- *20g mango*

FOR THE DRESSING:

- *50g mango*
- *1 tbsp hemp or olive oil*
- *50ml water*
- *some parsley (fresh or dried)*
- *salt and pepper*

TOPPINGS:

- *1 small handful beansprouts*

Tip

* When it comes to raw vegetables, you need a really strong digestion – otherwise you might get stomach aches and bloating. Our digestion is usually weaker when we are stressed or travelling, so you should consider staying away from raw vegetables then!

1 Wash, clean and spin-dry the lettuce. Wash and clean the vegetables and fruit, peel if necessary. Process the zucchini in a spiral vegetable slicer to make zoodles. Grate the carrots, slice the beetroot into a super thin 'carpaccio', cut the cucumber into sticks, the red radishes in halves and dice the mango.

2 For the mango dressing, purée all the listed ingredients until creamy and season with salt and pepper. You can also use frozen mango for this part – just defrost it beforehand in this case.

3 Now the most 'difficult' step: Place the lettuce in a bowl and the fruit and veggies on top – making it look like a rainbow – pretty similar to the stripes on an açai bowl! Top with the beansprouts.

Why is 'raw' such a hot topic? Various nutrients can be very sensitive to heat and therefore destroyed when cooked. Non-heated foods contain, for example, more vitamin B and C. Some antioxidants can be lost completely – which would be a real shame! That's why you should treat yourself by eating fresh and crunchy vegetables from time to time. Still, the healthy properties can only unfold if you are able to actually digest the foods. Trial and error is the way to go – some are rather sensitive, some are not. Personally, I tend to struggle with raw broccoli, cauliflower and kale. But cucumber, radish and carrots are perfectly fine for me!

NUTRITIONAL VALUES APPROX. 192 KCAL – 4G PROTEIN – 22G CARBOHYDRATES – 4G FIBRE – 10G FAT (8G UNSATURATED)

VEGGIE STICKS
with Hummus – The Quick Snack

about 15 mins

FOR THE VEGETABLE STICKS:

- *1 carrot*
- *1/2 cucumber*
- *1/2 pepper*
- *1 tomato*
- *1 handful radishes*

FOR THE HUMMUS:

- *80g canned chickpeas*
- *1 tbsp tahini*
- *1 tbsp olive oil or 1 tbsp plant milk*
- *1 big splash of lemon juice*
- *1/2 tsp ground cumin*
- *1 big pinch of salt*
- *pepper*
- *optional: garlic*

Tip

* A lot of antioxidants are located right beneath the skin. That's why I don't peel my vegetables if it's not really necessary – washing them thoroughly is sufficient for organic foods!

1 Wash and clean the vegetables, peel if needed. Cut the carrot, cucumber and pepper into sticks; the tomatoes and radishes are either cut in halves or quarters.

2 For the hummus, rinse the chickpeas under running water in a sieve, drain, shell them if you like to and then purée with the remaining ingredients until creamy. Classically that's olive oil but if you prefer a calorie-reduced version you can also use your favourite plant milk!

3 Usually you need to assist your blender or food processor by pushing the mixture back down towards the blade. Just make sure the hummus turns out nice and creamy.

4 Arrange the vegetables nicely and serve the hummus in a bowl. Perfect to share – if you are willing to.

An easy snack that only takes a minute to prepare. This mouth-watering savoury snack is rich in both proteins and healthy fats. Hummus, thank God, not only tastes great with flatbread but also – or maybe even better – with vegetables. This combination provides us with a lot of vitamins, minerals and a big bunch of fibre and antioxidants. Ideal as a snack between meals, to share or as a starter!
PS: Check out my other hummus versions on page 216!

NUTRITIONAL VALUES APPROX. 338 KCAL – 12G PROTEIN – 31G CARBOHYDRATES – 12G FIBRE – 17G FAT (14G UNSATURATED)

QUICK VEGGIE SOUP
with Spinach, Peas & Cashews

about 10 mins
+ 2 hrs. soaking

- *30g cashew nuts*
- *salt*
- *250ml cashew milk*
- *70g spinach (fresh or frozen)*
- *70g peas (fresh or frozen)*
- *1 splash of lemon juice*
- *1–2 tsp agave syrup*
- *pepper*
- *grated nutmeg*
- *chilli powder*

TOPPINGS:

- *fresh basil, peas*

Info

* The iron contained in *spinach* can be absorbed much more effectively when paired with vitamin C, so don't forget the splash of lemon!

1 Optional: Soak the cashew nuts for at least 2 hours, or even overnight, in a glass of water with a little salt. Afterwards, place them in a sieve and rinse them with water. This helps with the following steps and also makes the cashew nuts easier to digest.

2 Purée the cashew nuts, cashew milk, spinach and peas until creamy. If you have fresh basil at hand, feel free to toss that in as well

3 Season the soup with the lemon juice, agave syrup, salt, pepper and the spices.

4 Slowly heat up the soup in a saucepan on the stove and season again if needed. Garnish with basil and a few peas. Done!

This soup scores the highest in terms of convenience and time needed. Mixing and heating – that's it! It doesn't necessarily require fresh ingredients so you can keep everything in stock. I always keep spinach and peas in the freezer; cashew milk can be stored unopened (and even uncooled!) for about a year; and the rest can usually be found in most store cupboards too!

NUTRITIONAL VALUES APPROX. 342 KCAL – 15G PROTEIN – 24G CARBOHYDRATES – 6G FIBRE – 21G FAT (17G UNSATURATED)

CREAMY SQUASH SOUP
with Coconut & Ginger

about 25 mins

- *200g Hokkaido squash*
- *3–4 thin slices of ginger (alternative: ground ginger)*
- *200ml plant milk (e.g. almond milk)*
- *50ml creamy coconut milk (about 60% coconut)*
- *salt*
- *pepper*
- *grated nutmeg*

TOPPINGS:

- *10g pumpkin seeds, 1 tsp coconut milk*

1 Peel the squash and remove the seeds. Cut it into pieces. Peel the ginger and mince as finely as possible. Alternatively, you can use ground ginger.

2 In a saucepan, let the squash and ginger simmer in a mixture of the plant milk, creamy coconut milk and a pinch of salt. Depending on the size of the pieces, the time to cook may vary. Usually it takes around 15 minutes. I simply wait until I can divide the pieces with a cooking spoon – that's my indicator that they are soft enough!

3 Purée everything and season with the salt, pepper and nutmeg. If the consistency is too thick, you can add some more plant milk.

4 Dress with pumpkin seeds and coconut milk – enjoy!

Squash meets coconut … never tried that combination before? Then it's about time! A creamy squash soup is an absolute classic in my kitchen. I especially enjoy these warming dishes as soon as autumn arrives. Coconut milk is a perfect plant-based alternative to cream or crème fraîche – and one that tastes even better in my opinion!

NUTRITIONAL VALUES APPROX. 313 KCAL – 11G PROTEIN – 32G CARBOHYDRATES – 5G FIBRE – 16G FAT (4G UNSATURATED)

Sweet Bowls

5

Skipping dessert, just because you're trying to eat more healthily? Well, you don't have to! That's why I'm not leaving out the sweet bowls in my book. Hot coconut banana pie, brownies or ice cream – feel free to indulge your sweet tooth without having a bad conscience. And there's a reason: not all sugars are created equal! With natural ingredients you can easily cook wonderful desserts or snacks that work out great without any refined sugar or white flour. I achieve this by working with the natural sweetness of whole fruits and with nutritious, high-quality sugars like coconut blossom sugar, honey or date syrup. Our body digests these sugars less quickly and your blood sugar levels will therefore not go on a rollercoaster ride. Using whole, natural ingredients is super important to me in this chapter as well, so I don't use any artificial sweeteners or chemical substitutes in my recipes.

COOKIE DOUGH CREAM

about 10 mins

- *150g canned chickpeas*
- *80g ripe banana*
- *30g hazelnut butter (alternative: a different nut butter, e.g. peanut butter)*
- *6–8 tbsp water*
- *vanilla powder*
- *salt*
- *20g vegan chocolate chips (minimum 80% cocoa)*
- *optional: agave, date syrup or coconut blossom sugar*

1 For this recipe I use canned chickpeas. Rinse them under running water and shell them if you like to (benefits of shelling on page 31).

2 Blend the chickpeas with the ripe banana and the hazelnut butter until smooth.

3 Start adding tablespoons of water, keep mixing and stop when you reach a creamy consistency.

4 Season with the vanilla and salt. If the sweetness of the banana isn't strong enough for your liking, add some more banana or alternatively one of the listed sweeteners.

5 Carefully stir in the chocolate chips and put the cream into the fridge for at least 1 hour.

Everyone who tried the Cookie Dough Cream while I was perfecting the recipe for this book came to the same conclusion: sooo delicious! This is for sure not a light and airy dish, but lovely, rich and creamy. Perfect for all those moments when you can't resist the cravings. My brother was missing sweetness in the base recipe. If you agree with him, you can easily adjust the taste by adding agave or date syrup. Bon appétit!

Tip

* Looking for a healthier alternative to the *chocolate chips*? Simple: cocoa nibs!

NUTRITIONAL VALUES APPROX. 598 KCAL – 17G PROTEIN – 47G CARBOHYDRATES – 15G FIBRE – 35G FAT (25G UNSATURATED)

NICE CREAM – 4 *Flavours*

about 10 minutes

For all creams:

1 Peel the ripe bananas, slice and freeze for a minimum of 3 hours. I put the slices in plastic bags, but I clean and reuse them to minimize my plastic waste.

2 If you already store bananas in your freezer – which I highly recommend – defrost them for about 5 to 10 minutes before cooking.

Probably one of the best ideas that health freaks ever invented: using the creamy consistency of bananas to create the base for ice cream! With this trick you can create delicious ice cream in various flavours. It's vegan, without any dairy or refined sugar. The banana provides so much natural sweetness, I can easily leave out the note 'optional: agave or date syrup' for this recipe.

Tip

* Always prepare fresh! This recipe is not suitable for storing the ice cream in the fridge. But this does not matter too much since cooking takes 2 minutes max.

CHOCOLATE:

- *200g frozen banana (about 2 whole bananas)*
- *4 tsp raw, low-fat cocoa powder*

TOPPINGS:
- *1 tsp cocoa nibs*

Chocolate

Blend the frozen banana slices and the cocoa powder until creamy. A food processor or high-speed blender works best for this. Sprinkle with the cocoa nibs.

NUTRITIONAL VALUES APPROX. 285 KCAL – 7G PROTEIN – 49G CARBOHYDRATES – 6G FIBRE – 5G FAT (2G UNSATURATED)

STRAWBERRY-COCONUT:

- *150g frozen banana*
- *100g frozen strawberries*
- *20ml creamy coconut milk (about 60% coconut)*

TOPPINGS:

- *1 tsp grated coconut*

Strawberry-Coconut

Blend the banana and strawberries with the coconut milk. Dress with grated coconut.

NUTRITIONAL VALUES APPROX. 244 KCAL – 3G PROTEIN – 41G CARBOHYDRATES – 7G FIBRE – 8G FAT (1G UNSATURATED)

CRUNCHY ALMOND:

- *20g chopped almonds*
- *200g frozen banana*
- *3 tsp almond butter*

Crunchy Almond

Definitely my favourite flavour! Chop the almonds, mix 3/4 of them with the frozen banana and almond butter in a blender. Top the ice cream with the remaining chopped almonds and enjoy.

NUTRITIONAL VALUES APPROX. 469 KCAL – 12G PROTEIN – 51G CARBOHYDRATES – 10G FIBRE – 25G FAT (22G UNSATURATED)

CARAMEL:

- *2 stoned dates*
- *200g frozen banana*
- *3 tsp hazelnut butter (alternative: peanut butter)*
- *vanilla powder*
- *1 big pinch of salt*

Caramel

Shred one date in a blender. Then add the banana, hazelnut butter, vanilla and salt. Chop the second date and add it to your ice cream. Top with chopped dates.

NUTRITIONAL VALUES APPROX. 478 KCAL – 7G PROTEIN – 75G CARBOHYDRATES – 11G FIBRE – 16G FAT (14G UNSATURATED)

BAKED ALMOND CRUMBLE *with Fruits*

about 50 mins

FOR THE FRUIT MIX:

- *1 nectarine*
- *1 pear*
- *1 fig*
- *1 plum*
- *50g apple purée*

FOR THE CRUMBLE:

- *20g almonds*
- *30g oats*
- *10g ground almonds*
- *10g almond flour*
- *40ml almond milk*
- *1 tsp date syrup*
- *1 pinch of salt*
- *1 tsp ground Ceylon cinnamon*
- *1 tsp coconut oil*

... Food Swaps ...

* You can use almost all kinds of fruit! Simply pick what's in season: apple, pear, plum, or grapes – I've successfully tried them all.

1 Preheat the oven to 160°C.

2 Wash, stone and/or peel the fruit as needed, cut them into pieces and mix with the apple purée in a bowl.

3 For the crumble, roughly chop the almonds and knead with all the remaining ingredients (except the coconut oil) to create a dough.

4 Grease an ovenproof dish with the coconut oil and place the fruit in it. Crumble the dough and place the crumbs loosely on top of the fruit.

5 Bake for 30–40 minutes in the preheated oven and serve while still hot.

Actually, this is the first recipe picture I shot for this book. I hope you *can't* tell. I spent a whopping 30 minutes taking photos of this bowl to make sure I had the perfect shot. Anyway, this bowl tastes best when still hot and fresh from the oven. But I can assure you – after those 30 minutes – it's also pretty good when cold. The crumble on top surprises me again and again: simple, very natural and incredibly delicious.

NUTRITIONAL VALUES APPROX. 595 KCAL – 19G PROTEIN – 73G CARBOHYDRATES – 17G FIBRE – 26G FAT (18G UNSATURATED)

THE

BAKED BERRY BOWL
with Chocolate-Coconut Crumble

about 25 mins

- *30g oats*
- *10g coconut flour*
- *10g coconut flakes*
- *1 tsp raw, low-fat cocoa powder*
- *1 pinch of salt*
- *40ml creamy coconut milk (about 60% coconut)*
- *2 tsp coconut oil*
- *1 tsp date syrup*
- *150g frozen or fresh berries*

NUTRITIONAL VALUES APPROX.

406 KCAL – 10G PROTEIN – 33G CARBOHYDRATES – 16G FIBRE – 23G FAT (4G UNSATURATED)

1 Preheat the oven to 180°C.

2 In a bowl, mix the oats, coconut flour, coconut flakes, cocoa powder and salt.

3 To the dry ingredients, add the coconut milk, 1 tsp of the coconut oil and date syrup. Knead to create a dough.

4 Grease an ovenproof dish with the remaining coconut oil. Put a couple of berries aside. Place the rest of the berries in the bowl. Crumble the dough and sprinkle it on top of the berries. Don't flatten it out though, a rough, uneven surface is intended!

5 Place the remaining berries on top of the chocolate dough – we want it to look appealing in the end. Bake for 15 minutes and enjoy straight from the dish!

This baked crumble is THE FAVOURITE recipe of Anna – the photographer who shot all the pictures of me in this book. Initially, this wasn't even a recipe but just a way to make use of all the leftovers at the end of a photo shoot. She was so amazed by it, I had to bake it again and again whenever we changed location! So, it became obvious to me: this crumble is so much more than just using up scraps. Sometimes unplanned things turn out to be the best.

AUSTRIAN QUINOA-ALMOND
Kaiserschmarrn with Homemade Jam

about 30 mins

- *40g uncooked quinoa*
- *salt*
- *1 egg*
- *1 tsp crushed flaxseeds*
- *vanilla powder*
- *1 tbsp coconut blossom sugar (sweeter option: 2 tbsp)*
- *50ml plant milk*
- *20g almonds*
- *20g raisins*
- *1 tsp coconut oil*

TOPPINGS:

- *50g Sugar-free Berry Jam (find the recipe on page 213), 1 tsp grated coconut*

NUTRITIONAL VALUES APPROX.

564 KCAL – 21G PROTEIN – 57G CARBOHYDRATES – 10G FIBRE – 27G FAT (17G UNSATURATED)

1 Prepare the Berry Jam for the topping (please find the instructions on page 213)

2 Rinse the quinoa in a sieve. Let it simmer with 2.5 times the volume of water and a pinch of salt until the water is absorbed completely.

3 Meanwhile, mix the egg, flaxseeds, a pinch of salt, vanilla and coconut blossom sugar. Add the quinoa and plant milk to the egg mixture and blend to create a batter. The consistency of the batter does not need to be very thick. Chop the almonds and stir into the batter with the raisins.

4 In a frying pan, heat the coconut oil and make a pancake with the batter. As soon as it slides from side to side when tilting the pan, you can flip the pancake. Fry both sides until golden brown. Then, use your spatula to divide the pancake into bite-sized pieces, place these in a bowl and serve with grated coconut and jam.

Wondering what a 'Kaiserschmarrn' is? It's a well-known dessert in Austria and resembles a shredded pancake. Just thinking about it reminds me of ski trips and gets me drooling. My recipe would probably not be served at ski lodges due to all the changes I have made – it's just too far from the authentic version. No flour, no butter and no icing sugar. Instead there are nutrient-dense quinoa, crispy almonds and homemade jam.

FRIED APPLE
with Apple-Pie Cream

about 15 mins

FOR THE APPLE-PIE CREAM:

- *50g canned chickpeas*
- *50g apple*
- *1 tsp nut butter (e.g. cashew or almond)*
- *2 tbsp plant milk (e.g. cashew)*
- *1 tsp ground Ceylon cinnamon*
- *1 pinch of salt*
- *some grated nutmeg*
- *1/2 tsp ground ginger*
- *10g raisins*

FOR THE COCONUT-FRIED APPLE:

- *1 apple*
- *1 tsp coconut oil*
- *1/2 tsp ground Ceylon cinnamon*
- *1 dash of water*
- *50g plant yoghurt (e.g. cashew or coconut)*

1 To make the apple-pie cream, thoroughly rinse the chickpeas, peel and core the apple. In a blender, mix the chickpeas, the apple and all the remaining ingredients (except the raisins) until smooth. Add the raisins only at the end. The cream tends to stick to the sides of the blender, so you usually need to help by pushing the mixture back down towards the blade.

2 For the fried apple, wash and core the apple, cut it into pieces and in a frying pan, sauté it with the coconut oil and cinnamon. Add a dash of water so that the cinnamon spreads more evenly and the apple pieces become nice and soft. Too much oil would tamper with the flavour – so use water instead!

3 Serve the fried apple with the apple-pie cream and a yoghurt of your choice – I like cashew and coconut the best.

For all those times when you crave something sweet but don't feel like chocolate … rather something light and fruity. This bowl reminds of grandma's apple pie – without being a pie. I admit, this delicacy is hard to define. The bowl combines the flavours of apple pie while being a cream combined with a fried apple. This bowl tastes satisfying and delicious but is totally guilt-free! There is no added sugar.

NUTRITIONAL VALUES APPROX. 298 KCAL – 7G PROTEIN – 36G CARBOHYDRATES – 8G FIBRE – 12G FAT (7G UNSATURATED)

Fruits with Chocolate-Avocado Dip & SWEET HUMMUS

about 25 mins

CHOCOLATE-AVOCADO DIP:

- *100g avocado*
- *1/2 very ripe banana*
- *3 tsp raw, low-fat cocoa powder*
- *2–3 tbsp plant milk*

NUTRITIONAL VALUES APPROX.
260 KCAL – 6G PROTEIN – 22G CARBOHYDRATES – 8G FIBRE – 17G FAT (12G UNSATURATED)

SWEET HUMMUS:

- *150g canned chickpeas*
- *2 stoned dates*
- *4–5 tbsp plant milk*
- *1/2 tsp ground Ceylon cinnamon*

NUTRITIONAL VALUES APPROX.
315 KCAL – 12G PROTEIN – 49G CARBOHYDRATES – 14G FIBRE – 5G FAT (4G UNSATURATED)

Perfect if you are having friends over and are in need of food that can be shared and looks great on the table! A wonderful creamy, rich chocolate dip that doesn't give you a hint of the avocado it contains, and an unconventional, sweet approach to the popular hummus. It is prepared with healthy ingredients like ripe bananas and dates – fruits are the sweets of nature. The banana and avocado should be as ripe as possible. This results in the dip not only being sweeter, but also way creamier!

Preparation: Wash, core, peel and/or cut the fruit of your preference (about 200g per person). Cut the fruit into bite-sized pieces so you can dip them easily.

Chocolate-Avocado Dip

Cut the avocado in half and remove the stone. Remove the flesh by using a spoon and mash it afterwards with a fork. Peel the banana and mash it with a fork as well. Mix both the mashed banana and the avocado. Add the cocoa powder and stir thoroughly. If the consistency is too thick or hard to mix, add some plant milk.

Sweet Hummus

Rinse the chickpeas thoroughly, shell them if you like. Shred the dates in a blender. Add the chickpeas, some plant milk and cinnamon and continue blending.

COCONUT BANANA CAKE
with Chocolate Pieces

about 30–40 mins

- *1 tsp coconut oil*
- *1 egg*
- *2 pinches of salt*
- *2 tbsp coconut flour*
- *1 tbsp grated coconut*
- *1 (brown) banana (about 100g)*
- *vanilla powder*
- *10g dark, vegan chocolate*
- *optional: 1 tsp coconut blossom sugar*

TOPPINGS:

- *10g dark vegan chocolate, some grated coconut*

Tip

* I love overly ripe, brown *bananas*! They're not only sweeter and contain more antioxidants but are also well suited to baking. If you only have fresh, yellow bananas at hand, you can bake these in their peel in the oven for 20 minutes at 160°C. This speeds up the process of ripening and they turn brown in no time.

1 Preheat the oven to 180°C. Grease an ovenproof dish with some coconut oil.

2 Separate the egg and beat the egg white with a pinch of salt until stiff. Mix the coconut flour with the grated coconut and a pinch of salt.

3 In a separate bowl, blend the egg yolk with half of the banana and some vanilla powder until you have a smooth mixture. Sweeten with coconut blossom sugar if you like, then stir in the dry flour mix.

4 Cut the remaining banana and chocolate into pieces and carefully fold them into the dough with the beaten egg white. Immediately pour the batter into the prepared dish. Top with more chocolate, banana pieces and grated coconut. Bake for 20–30 minutes.

A cake to spoon straight from your bowl. Of all the sweet recipes, this banana cake is my parents' absolute favourite. The method of separating and beating the egg white until stiff results in a great light and airy texture – without a grain of baking powder. We have always done it that way at home, for every single cake!

NUTRITIONAL VALUES APPROX. 436 KCAL – 14G PROTEIN – 33G CARBOHYDRATES – 12G FIBRE – 25G FAT (6G UNSATURATED)

CARROT CAKE BOWL
with Crunchy Almond Nice Cream

about 35 mins

FOR THE CAKE:

- *1 tsp coconut oil*
- *1 egg*
- *salt*
- *2 tbsp spelt flour*
- *1/2 tsp ground Ceylon cinnamon*
- *1/4 tsp ground ginger*
- *some grated nutmeg*
- *1–3 tsp coconut blossom sugar*
- *1 carrot (about 70g)*
- *2 tbsp plant milk*
- *20g nuts*
- *10g raisins*

TOPPINGS:

- *Crunchy Almond Nice Cream (instructions on page 177. Amounts: 10g chopped almonds, 50g frozen banana, 1 tsp almond butter)*

TOTAL: 512 KCAL – 17G PROTEIN – 50G CARBOHYDRATES – 10G FIBRE – 27G FAT (21G UNSATURATED)

1 Preheat the oven to 180°C. Grease an ovenproof dish with some coconut oil. For the cake, separate the egg and beat the egg white with a pinch of salt until stiff.

2 Mix the spelt flour with the cinnamon, ginger, nutmeg, coconut blossom sugar and some salt.

3 Peel the carrot and either grate it by hand or shred it with a food processor. Combine with the plant milk and egg yolk.

4 Blend together both the flour (from step 2) and carrot mix (from step 3). Chop the nuts and stir them into the batter with the raisins. Gently fold in the beaten egg white and pour the batter into the prepared dish immediately. Bake for about 20 minutes in the preheated oven.

5 In the meantime, make the Crunchy Almond Nice Cream (please find the instructions on page 177) and serve with the cake.

A cookbook without a carrot cake wouldn't be 'my cookbook'. I love it with my whole heart and I just can't get enough of this spicy-sweet interplay of flavours.

CAKE: 362 KCAL – 13G PROTEIN – 36G CARBOHYDRATES – 7G FIBRE – 18G FAT (13G UNSATURATED)
CRUNCHY-ALMOND NICE CREAM: 150 KCAL – 4G PROTEIN – 14G CARBOHYDRATES – 3G FIBRE – 9G FAT (8G UNSATURATED)

OAT COOKIE BOWL
with Blueberries

about 30–40 mins

- *1 tsp coconut oil*
- *50g rolled oats*
- *1 tsp crushed flaxseeds*
- *1 tsp coconut blossom sugar (for a sweeter variation: 2–3 tsp)*
- *1 pinch of salt*
- *1 tsp ground nuts (e.g. almonds)*
- *1 tsp peanut butter (salted)*
- *50g yoghurt (e.g. cashew or coconut yoghurt)*
- *1 handful of blueberries (fresh or frozen)*

TOPPINGS:

- *1 tsp peanut butter*

Note

* Recommended to all porridge lovers!

1 Preheat the oven to 180°C. Grease an ovenproof dish with some coconut oil.

2 In a bowl, mix the oats, crushed flaxseeds, coconut blossom sugar, salt and ground nuts. Then add the peanut butter and knead to create a dough. If you are using unsalted peanut butter, feel free to add some additional salt.

3 Fold in the coconut yoghurt and, as the very last ingredient, the blueberries. Pour the dough into the bowl. Just let it drop in there kind of loosely, it does not need to be pressed into the base of the bowl!

4 Bake in the preheated oven for 25–35 minutes until crispy. And how about some more peanut butter as a topping?

Oh well, the Oat Cookie Bowl. This recipe turned out to be a failure around 10 or 15 times until I finally figured out the right ingredients. I was dying to add my beloved oats as a cake or cookie in the Sweet Bowls chapter, ideally as a vegan dish without the use of eggs. After quite a number of attempts the winners were rolled oats, ground nuts and coconut yoghurt creating the perfect cookie bowl.

NUTRITIONAL VALUES APPROX. 395 KCAL – 14G PROTEIN – 42G CARBOHYDRATES – 9G FIBRE – 18G FAT (15G UNSATURATED)

The 'Sweet' SWEET POTATO

about 40–70 mins

- *1 medium sized sweet potato (about 200g)*

TOPPINGS:

- *10g pecans, 1 tsp cocoa nibs, some blackberries and raisins, Ceylon cinnamon and 2 tsp honey*

NUTRITIONAL VALUES APPROX.

366 KCAL – 5G PROTEIN – 62G CARBOHYDRATES – 9G FIBRE – 11G FAT (8G UNSATURATED)

Info

* The colour of *sweet potatoes* originates from beta-carotene. Our body transforms it into vitamin A, which supports your eyesight and clear, beautiful skin. There's a reason that acne is often treated with medication containing vitamin A. Just 100g of sweet potato covers a multiple of its daily recommended intake!

1 Preheat the oven to 180°C.

2 Wash the sweet potato and prick the skin with a fork. Place the whole sweet potato on a baking tray lined with baking parchment and put it in the oven.

3 Depending on its size, the sweet potato might take 30 to 60 minutes until done. To check, simply use a knife and test if it glides easily into the potato.

4 Take the potato out of the oven, cut it lengthwise and break open. To create a fluffy consistency, loosen the flesh with a fork.

5 Garnish the sweet potato with whatever your heart desires. I love raisins, pecans, cocoa nibs, berries, cinnamon and honey.

6 The sweet potato tastes best when hot – you can either spoon it out or eat the peel as well.

My definition of simple, natural food. This recipe is the proof that sweet potatoes not only taste great along with savoury flavours, but also mind-blowing with sweet ingredients. For a vegan version you can use maple syrup instead of honey.

Creamy Zucchini & Apple BROWNIE BOWL

about 2 hrs.

- *1 tsp coconut oil*
- *1 tsp ground flaxseeds*
- *30g peanut, almond or coconut flour*
- *1 big pinch of salt*
- *2 tsp raw, low-fat cocoa powder*
- *80g zucchini*
- *2–3 stoned dates*
- *50g apple purée*
- *vanilla powder*
- *50g apple*

TOPPINGS:

- *1 tsp cocoa nibs, 1 tsp chopped hazelnuts, 1 tsp date syrup*

Info

* This bowl provides almost 50% of the daily recommended intake of fibre! Fibre encourages digestion, keeps you satiated and maintains a healthy gut flora.

1 Preheat the oven to 180°C. Grease an ovenproof dish with coconut oil.

2 Let the flaxseeds soak and swell in twice their volume of hot water. Mix the flour with the salt and cocoa powder. Wash the zucchini and either shred it in a food processor or grate it by hand.

3 Using a blender or food processor, shred the dates until they become a smooth paste. Add the apple purée, vanilla and soaked flaxseeds and blend again. Then in a bowl, knead the zucchini, flour mix and date paste to create a dough. Clean and cut the apple in small pieces and fold into the dough. Set aside some pieces for the topping.

4 Pour the dough into the prepared dish and garnish with the cocoa nibs, chopped hazelnuts and apple pieces. Bake for about 40 minutes and let it cool for at least 1 hour afterwards. Drizzle some date syrup on top before serving.

This recipe is quite light, creamy and has a nice sweetness to it. It's definitely not a sinful sugar bomb, since we're only using dates to sweeten. Wonder why we are using a zucchini at all? To make it light, voluminous and soft – without affecting the flavours!

NUTRITIONAL VALUES APPROX. 430 KCAL – 23G PROTEIN – 49G CARBOHYDRATES – 14G FIBRE – 12G FAT (7G UNSATURATED)

Chocolate & Bean
BROWNIE BOWL

about 30–40 mins

- *1 tsp coconut oil*
- *10g crushed flaxseeds*
- *200g canned black beans*
- *3 tsp raw, low-fat coconut powder*
- *1 big pinch of salt*
- *vanilla powder*
- *30g date syrup*

(for a sweeter variation: 40–50g)

TOPPINGS:

- *20g vegan dark chocolate chips, 10g pecans*

NUTRITIONAL VALUES APPROX.

541 KCAL – 17G PROTEIN – 53G CARBOHYDRATES – 16G FIBRE – 24G FAT (11G UNSATURATED)

1 Preheat the oven to 180°C. Grease an ovenproof dish with some coconut oil.

2 Let the crushed flaxseeds soak and swell in twice their volume of hot water. Meanwhile, rinse the black beans and then blend with the cocoa powder, salt, a little vanilla and date syrup until a smooth dough is created. Add the soaked flaxseeds and stir.

3 Pour the brownie dough into the prepared dish, sprinkle with the chocolate chips and nuts and bake for 20–30 minutes. Remove it from the oven and enjoy!

Does it taste the way it looks? YES! I am repeatedly surprised by how you can create a convincing brownie texture by using black beans. Admittedly, I am not the only person to appreciate this fact – bean brownies are very popular, especially among vegans. Since black beans provide a lot of great dietary benefits but no sweetness whatsoever, just add a generous amount of date syrup. Alternatively, you can also use coconut blossom sugar. So, don't be afraid: beans definitely are suitable for sweet dishes – I promise!

Food Swaps: Black beans work best – but if you can't find them at your supermarket, feel free to go for kidney beans.

Side Bowls

6

In this chapter I have collected all my favourite recipes for sides, toppings and dips – perfect additions to round off the bowl recipes. You can also find foods that you would usually buy from the supermarket like jam or granola. You can prepare these in just a couple of minutes. What's so great about that? You know exactly what ingredients went in – and ensure that they are high quality!

ULTIMATE RAWNOLA

Preparation:

1 Fill a glass with water, mix in the lemon juice or apple cider vinegar. Add thebuckwheat and let it soak overnight. Rinse thoroughly in the morning since the grains will have produced some slime. Let it dry completely on paper towels.

2 Let the nuts and seeds soak as well, ideally overnight or for at least 6 hours, in water and a bit of salt. Afterwards rinse and dry.

3 Either you let the flaxseeds (whole or crushed) soak with twice the amount of water for a couple of hours, or go for the quick version with hot water. That way it takes about 10 minutes until they swell and get slimy. There is no need to rinse the flaxseeds afterwards.

about 15 mins + soaking overnight

SERVING: 150G

- *1 tsp lemon juice or apple cider vinegar*
- *20g buckwheat, uncooked*
- *30g nuts (e.g. almonds and cashews)*
- *10g larger seeds (e.g. pumpkin and sunflower seeds)*
- *salt*
- *2 stoned dates*
- *10g coconut flakes*
- *1 tsp ground Ceylon cinnamon*
- *10g smaller seeds (e.g. flaxseeds and hemp seeds)*
- *vanilla powder*
- *10g dried berries (e.g. mulberries)*
- *10g puffed quinoa or oats*

Tip

* If you tend to have trouble digesting nuts and seeds, you can soak them for every recipe. This helps to make them easier to digest.

Cooking:

1 Process the dates into a smooth paste with a food processor or blender.

2 Add the buckwheat, nuts, larger seeds, coconut flakes, cinnamon and vanilla and mix until the ingredients are mixed evenly and the nuts are chopped up roughly.

3 Then add the smaller seeds, berries and puffed quinoa – as an alternative to the quinoa you can also use oats. If you like the Rawnola pieces to be small, process for a short time. If you prefer them bigger, just stir by hand.

4 Depending on how dry the buckwheat and nuts were when adding, the consistency of the Rawnola may vary. If it's too moist, spread it on a tray lined with baking parchment and let it sit in a well-ventilated spot. A dehydrator can also be used! Then, store in a sealed jar in a cool place and enjoy within a week.

Yes, it takes some preparation, but you get the Ultimate Rawnola with an unbeatable number of health advantages. Nuts, seeds and grains are very high in fibre. However, they do contain anti-nutrients which can cause tummy-aches or bloating. Soaking in advance helps neutralize those anti-nutrients, ensuring absorption of 'good nutrients'.

NUTRITIONAL VALUES PER 100G APPROX. 385 KCAL – 11G PROTEIN – 39G CARBOHYDRATES – 7G FIBRE – 19G FAT (14G UNSATURATED)

FRUITY RAWNOLA – *In under 10 Minutes!*

about 10 mins

SERVING: 150G

- *10g crushed flaxseeds*
- *2 tbsp hot water*
- *2 stoned dates*
- *40g oats*
- *20g goji berries*
- *20g dried apple rings*
- *10g cocoa nibs*
- *1 big pinch of salt*
- *1 big pinch of ground Ceylon cinnamon*

PER 100G APPROX.
332 KCAL – 8G PROTEIN – 54G CARBOHYDRATES – 14G FIBRE – 9G FAT (6G UNSATURATED)

Tip

* The Rawnola can be served immediately but it tastes better on the second day, since it dries and loses moisture.

1 Let the crushed flaxseeds soak in the hot water for 5 minutes. In the meantime, turn the dates into a smooth paste using a food processor or blender. If they are too hard, you can soak them in water first.

2 Combine half of the oats, the soaked flaxseeds and the date paste either in a food processor or regular kitchen mixer – a blender would cut the ingredients too finely. Mix them evenly.

3 Add in the remaining ingredients and mix until the desired consistency is reached. The longer you do so, the more homogenous it will get. I prefer to have some bigger pieces in my Rawnola.

4 Either serve and enjoy immediately, or you can let the Rawnola sit and dry in the sun for 1–2 hours. If you own a dehydrator, you can use that of course! Then – if there is some Rawnola left – store in a sealed jar in the fridge. I don't want to take any responsibility for it, but my Rawnola stays perfect for 1–2 weeks.

Everybody should be familiar with GRANOLA, and a Rawnola is just its uncooked, raw sibling. As a result, all the nutrients and vitamins stay intact, which otherwise would be destroyed by the heat. I also used this one for the 'Rawnola Bowl' breakfast dish on page 79.

Oven-Baked VEGGIE CHIPS

about 30 mins

- *100g zucchini*
- *100g raw beetroot*
- *100g carrots*
- *100g sweet potato*
- *some avocado or coconut oil*
- *salt and pepper*
- *sweet paprika*

NUTRITIONAL VALUES APPROX.

238 KCAL – 5G PROTEIN – 42G CARBOHYDRATES – 9G FIBRE – 5G FAT (3G UNSATURATED)

Tip

* Vegetables that contain a lot of water (e.g. zucchini) should be dried with paper towels prior to baking. For dryer vegetables (e.g. beetroot, sweet potatoes) cut the slices a little bit thicker (2–3mm). From my experience I'd recommend slicing carrots rather thinly.

1 Preheat the oven to 200°C.

2 Clean the raw vegetables, peel if you need to and cut them into very thin slices.

3 Coat the slices with a little oil – I usually use a pastry brush. Make sure not to use too much oil. Otherwise the chips won't get crunchy. You can also leave out the oil completely. There is not a major difference in taste, but they will tend to burn more easily so watch out while baking!

4 Sprinkle them with the spices and salt and spread in an even layer on a baking sheet lined with baking parchment. The chips shouldn't overlap or cover each other.

5 Bake for 10 minutes in the oven – flip all the slices and bake again for 5–10 minutes. Keep an eye on them, especially in these final minutes! Some can take longer or be ready more quickly depending on the thickness of your slices.

Craving a snack while watching TV in the evening? No problem, even if the shops are closed. Simply use vegetables (that you hopefully have in stock anyway) to create chips. They don't really taste like vegetables and are surely not a reason to feel bad!

Potato & Sweet Potato OVEN FRIES

about 40–50 mins

- *200g sweet potatoes*
- *200g potatoes*
- *3 tsp avocado or coconut oil*
- *salt*
- *pepper*
- *sweet paprika*
- *ground cumin*
- *chilli powder*

PER 100G APPROX.
138 KCAL – 2G PROTEIN –
20G CARBOHYDRATES –
3G FIBRE –
6G FAT (4G UNSATURATED)

Info

* *Sweet potatoes* do contain more sugar, but they still have a lower glycaemic index and more fibre than usual potatoes. This causes your blood sugar level to stay more stable and keeps you full for a longer period of time.

1 Preheat the oven to 180°C.

2 Clean and, if necessary, peel the potatoes. Cut them into long strips and toss them with a little avocado or coconut oil in a bowl. Beware, the more the merrier does not apply in this instance. If you use too much oil the fries won't turn out crispy but rather soggy!

3 In terms of spices, just go with the taste you prefer. You can find some classics in the ingredients list. Add these to the bowl and give it a toss.

4 Spread the fries evenly on a baking tray lined with baking parchment. Ideally, they won't touch or overlap. Bake them for 30–40 minutes in the oven.

Well, who does not like them? The image of our beloved potatoes in a slim, long and crispy appearance – so obviously I'm talking about fries – has suffered thanks to the fast-food industry. And they are surely not a synonym for 'healthy food'. The reason for that is the most common way to cook them though – deep-frying in a huge amount of low quality oil.
In reality the potato is a great tuber vegetable which can be happily enjoyed when baked in the oven with only a little, high quality oil.
PS: No one has ever complained that my oven fries taste too healthy. Not even the male members of my family.

Sugar-Free
BERRY JAM

about 15 mins

SERVING: 300G

- *300g berries (frozen or fresh)*
- *3–4 tsp chia seeds (alternatively 2 tsp chia seeds and 2 tsp psyllium husks)*
- *1 splash of lemon juice*
- *optional: agave, maple or date syrup to taste*

PER 100G APPROX.
58 KCAL – 2G PROTEIN – 8G CARBOHYDRATES – 3G FIBRE – 1G FAT (1G UNSATURATED)

Info

* Store in the fridge. Once opened, consume within 3–4 days.

1 Heat the berries in a saucepan over low heat. Stir regularly and wait for the liquid to evaporate. Mash the bigger berries while stirring.

2 As soon as the berries turn into a purée, stir in the chia seeds and lemon juice. Let the mixture soak over low heat. Alternatively, you can swap half of the chia seeds for psyllium husks. But watch out, if you use too much the mixture tends to get rather sticky.

3 If you like it a little sweeter, just add in some sweetener like date syrup. Using 2–3 teaspoons, or even tablespoons, is still super-far from how much sugar is usually used in jams! Also, if you prefer a smooth jam without pieces, just purée it in a blender at this point.

4 Pour the hot jam into a jar, close and tighten it firmly. When cooling down a vacuum is created and the berry jam can be enjoyed for 1–2 weeks.

Normal jam appears to be fruity and healthy – but that's misleading. Both store-bought jam and even the classic homemade recipe from our grandparents usually contain 50% (!!) added sugar. A jam with 75% fruit content is rarely found. With my recipe you get a pretty similar texture thanks to the swelling powers of the seeds and their shells. Without the sugar our jam can't be kept for as long, but when it tastes that great it doesn't really matter, does it?

FIG & PECAN JAM

PER 100G APPROX. 336 KCAL – 5G PROTEIN – 30G CARBOHYDRATES – 7G FIBRE – 23G FAT (19G UNSATURATED)

about 15 mins

SERVING: 300G

- *90g pecans*
- *2–3 slices fresh ginger*
- *600g ripe, fresh figs*
- *1 splash of lemon juice*
- *optional: vanilla powder, ground Ceylon cinnamon, salt*

Note

* Unopened and stored in the fridge, the jam is good for about 4–5 weeks. When opened, enjoy within 3–4 days.

1. Chop the pecans and ginger slices. Peel the fresh figs and cut into pieces.

2. Heat the nuts, figs and ginger with the lemon juice on the stove on low heat. The figs will lose liquid quickly. Simply let everything simmer for 10 minutes and stir regularly. While stirring I also like to mash the figs, making sure the finished jam won't contain pieces that are too big.

3. Season with vanilla, cinnamon and a pinch of salt if you like.

4. While still hot, pour the mixture into a jar, close and tighten firmly. When cooling down the vacuum should pull in the lid. If this worked out correctly, you will hear a loud 'clack'-sound when you open the jar.

SPINACH, WALNUT & OLIVE PESTO

APPROX. 309 KCAL – 4G PROTEIN – 3G CARBOHYDRATES – 2G FIBRE – 31G FAT (26G UNSATURATED)

about 10 mins

SERVING: 100G

- *40g baby spinach*
- *20g stoned olives*
- *20g walnuts*
- *1.5 tbsp oil (e.g. olive oil, flaxseed or hemp oil)*
- *1 tsp lemon juice*
- *salt and pepper*
- *optional: 1 tsp yeast flakes or grated Parmesan cheese*

Note

* Use up in 3–4 days.

1. Wash the baby spinach, shake dry and tear roughly. Cut the olives into small pieces and chop the walnuts.

2. Add all the ingredients to a blender and mix thoroughly. If you prefer a nutty, crunchy consistency, add the walnuts a little later so you'll end up with some bigger nut pieces in your pesto.

3. The yeast flakes or Parmesan are not mandatory – but they are delicious!

4. Have a taste, season and store in a sealed jar in the fridge. I like the pesto even better on day 2! By waiting, the ingredients homogenize and the flavours infuse through the whole pesto.

HUMMUS – 5 FLAVOURS

about 10 mins

Take the chickpeas out of the can, rinse them thoroughly and shell them if you like to (benefits of shelling on page 31). Alternatively, let them soak overnight and cook them yourself. In a blender, mix the chickpeas with tahini, olive oil (for a low-calorie version you can use plant milk instead), lemon juice, salt, seasonings and optionally garlic until smooth. For the different flavours, add the listed extras and blend. Usually you need to help a little to keep the purée from sticking to the sides of the blender by pushing it down regularly. If the consistency is too dry, add another tablespoon of oil or plant milk.

CLASSIC:

WITH OLIVE OIL:
244 KCAL – 7G PROTEIN – 13G CARBOHYDRATES – 7G FIBRE – 16G FAT (15G UNSATURATED)

WITH PLANT MILK:
165 KCAL – 7G PROTEIN – 13G CARBOHYDRATES – 7G FIBRE – 8G FAT (8G UNSATURATED)

- *80g canned chickpeas*
- *1 tbsp tahini*
- *1 small tbsp olive oil or 1 tbsp plant milk*
- *1 big splash of lemon juice*
- *1 big pinch of salt*
- *1/2 tsp ground cumin*
- *pepper*
- *optional: garlic*

PORTION: EACH 100G

MEDITERRANEAN HUMMUS:

WITH OLIVE OIL:
259 KCAL –
6G PROTEIN –
10G CARBOHYDRATES –
6G FIBRE –
20G FAT
(18G UNSATURATED)

- *50g canned chickpeas*
- *1 tbsp tahini*
- *1 small tbsp olive oil or*
- *1 tbsp plant milk*
- *1 big splash of lemon juice*
- *1 big pinch of salt*
- *dried oregano*
- *dried rosemary*
- *pepper*
- *optional: garlic*
- *20g olives*
- *10g sun-dried tomatoes*

PINK HUMMUS:

WITH OLIVE OIL:
227 KCAL –
6G PROTEIN –
12G CARBOHYDRATES –
6G FIBRE –
16G FAT
(14G UNSATURATED)

- *60g canned chickpeas*
- *1 tbsp tahini*
- *1 small tbsp olive oil or 1 tbsp plant milk*
- *1 big splash of lemon juice*
- *1 big pinch of salt*
- *1/2 tsp ground cumin*
- *pepper*
- *optional: garlic*
- *20g beetroots (raw or cooked)*

PEA & CASHEW HUMMUS:

WITH OLIVE OIL:
229 KCAL –
8G PROTEIN –
15G CARBOHYDRATES –
6G FIBRE –
15G FAT
(12G UNSATURATED)

- *40g canned chickpeas*
- *1 tbsp cashew butter (alternatively use tahini)*
- *1 small tbsp olive oil or 1 tbsp plant milk*
- *1 big splash of lemon juice*
- *1 big pinch of salt*
- *1/2 tbsp ground cumin*
- *pepper*
- *optional: garlic*
- *40g peas (frozen or fresh)*

SWEET POTATO & GINGER HUMMUS:

WITH OLIVE OIL:
241 KCAL –
6G PROTEIN –
17G CARBOHYDRATES –
6G FIBRE –
16G FAT
(14G UNSATURATED)

- *50g canned chickpeas*
- *1 tbsp tahini*
- *1 small tbsp olive oil or 1 tbsp plant milk*
- *1 big splash of lemon juice*
- *1 big pinch of salt and pepper*
- *1/2 tbsp ground cumin*
- *3–4 thin ginger slices, minced (alternatively use ground ginger)*
- *optional: garlic*
- *30g sweet potatoes (cooked or steamed)*

DISCLAIMER

All nutritional advice and information in this book is based on current and scientific/nutritional findings. However, practice, laws and regulations all change, and the reader should obtain up to date professional advice on such issues. The information contained in this book is for general purposes only and is not meant to substitute professional dietary advice or treatment. In no circumstances can the publisher or the author accept any liability for any loss, injury of damage of any kind resulting from any error in or omission from the information contained in this book.

ACKNOWLEDGEMENTS

As you know, too many cooks spoil the broth …

… which would be somehow unfavourable when it comes to a cookbook. That's why only a small handful of people have helped me with this book. I owe my highest appreciation to these few though. **THANK YOU!**

I threw an angry look at my mum quite a few times, when she (once again) said 'I think you can do better with this recipe.' And sure, even though I would have preferred not to hear that sentence from time to time, our perfectionism turns out to be totally worth it in the end. But not only thanks for that, mum, also for your endurance checking and selecting all the pictures I took. I know veggie bowl picture number 100 and me standing in the garden picture number 200 looked almost identical … but I know I can trust a strong, well-founded opinion when I ask you. Even at two o'clock in the morning.

In this context I want to thank Anna as well, who took all the photos of me. Our friendship is a lot of fun – we couldn't have made it through picking and editing thousands of pictures otherwise. The cover picture especially was a little nightmare in itself. From the moment it was (randomly) taken, Anna stood up for the current cover photo. For me, it took two additional cover shoots to realise that Anna was right from the beginning.

Also my publisher, Community Editions, can't be praised enough. I don't think it's common practice to receive so much freedom, help and understanding, so I really appreciate our wonderful way of working together.

Special thanks also to my brother Dennis, and to Daniela, who have both super supportive roles in my life and are always there to watch another inspiring documentary. That's how our understanding and awareness of overfished oceans, plastic in everyday life and the problems with avocados grew.

And many thanks to you. Thank you for going on this journey about nutrition. I hope one or two pieces of information provoked some sort of 'aha!' effect. If you now cook along with some of the recipes, go for the local alternative at the supermarket or drop fish or meat once in a while to help the environment – I am perfectly happy. Even if your first cooking attempt isn't perfect, it's about having fun. I burn my food as well once in a while. No drama – a good reason to swing the cooking spoon again!

ABOUT PAMELA REIF

Pamela is one of the most influential fitness and lifestyle role models in Germany. At the age of 16 Pamela found her passion for strength training. At the same time, she discovered her love for photography and shared her first pictures on Instagram. Private snapshots quickly turned into photos about sports, nutrition and travelling.

With her YouTube account *Pamela Rf* and her Instagram account *pamela_rf* she now reaches a community of more than 5 million people who follow her daily life and her excitement about fitness. On her second account *pamgoesnuts* she shares her knowledge of healthy and natural nutrition, as well as her favourite recipes.

IMPRINT

YOU DESERVE THIS

Simple & Natural Recipes for a Healthy Lifestyle. Bowl Cookbook

Zülpicher Platz 9
50674 Cologne
Germany

Text: Pamela Reif
Food styling: Pamela Reif
Translation from German: Dennis Reif
Design & layout: BUCH & DESIGN Vanessa Weuffel
Typesetting: bookwise GmbH
Project manager: Yasmin Reddig, Sarah Völker
Editing: Sylvia Goulding, Lesley Robb

Picture credits: © Anna Heupel: cover, back cover (bl, cr), endpaper, pp2, 4, 6 (t, b), 10, 17, 46, 55, 63, 65, 93, 117, 149, 173, 176, 203, 218 (tl, cl, cr, bl, br), 219 (tl, tr, cl, c, cr, bl), 223, endpaper; © Daniela Unrau: p219 (br); © Pamela Reif: back cover (tr, br, cb), pp6 (c), 12, 31, 42, 43, 58, 66–90, 94–114, 118–146, 150–170, 174, 178–200, 204–216; © private: p218 (tr)

stock.adobe.com: (pp19, 20, 23, 24, 29, 35, 37, 39, 41, 45): ©aedkafl, ©Africa Studio, ©alb470hanohiki, ©Alessio Orr., ©amy_lv, ©anchietaxavier, ©Anton, ©Armando, ©ArTo, ©AZP, ©barmalini, ©bbivirys, ©beerfan, ©breakingthewalls, ©Brent Hofacker, ©Carly Hennigan, ©ChiccoDodiFC, ©Christian Jung, ©cooperr, ©Davizro Photography, ©denira, ©Diana Taliun, ©Emilija, ©fabiomax, ©francescodemarco, ©irina, ©Iuliia, ©jonnysek, ©Julia, ©juliasudnitskaya, ©kaliantye, ©kariphoto, ©kiboka, ©kuvona, ©lastfurianec, ©Leonid, ©Marco2811, ©MarekPhotoDesign.com, ©Markus Mainka, ©Melica, ©Metkalova, ©nata_vkusidey, ©Natalia Mylova, ©Natallia, ©Olaf Speier, ©olllinka2, ©Patrik Stedrak, ©Paul Pellegrino, ©peangdao, ©phanuwatnandee, ©pheeraphan, ©philippev, ©photocrew, ©pichaituns, ©Picture Partners, ©prapholl, ©r_andrei, ©Rahul, ©red13fotostudio, ©Sergey Skleznev, ©sotopiko, ©tarasylo, ©Tim UR, ©ufotopixl10, ©vpardi, ©womue, ©Worldwide, ©yanadjan, ©Zechal, ©Андрій Пограничний, ©Игорь Головнёв

t = top, c = centre, b = bottom, l = left, r = right

Production: Community Editions GmbH

ISBN 978-3-96096-108-6

Printed in Poland

www.community-editions.de

FSC
www.fsc.org
MIX
Paper from responsible sources
FSC® C106632